SHAKESPEARE'S

HISTORY OF

KING HENRY THE EIGHTH.

EDITED, WITH NOTES,

BY

WILLIAM J. ROLFE, A.M.,

FORMERLY HEAD MASTER OF THE HIGH SCHOOL, CAMBRIDGE, MASS.

WITH ENGRAVINGS.

NEW YORK:

HARPER & BROTHERS, PUBLISHERS,

FRANKLIN SQUARE.

1872.

Entered according to Act of Congress, in the year 1871, by

Harper & Brothers,

In the Office of the Librarian of Congress, at Washington

PREFACE.

THIS edition of *Henry the Eighth* has been prepared on the same plan as those of *The Merchant of Venice* and *The Tempest*, and I have little to add by way of preface beyond a grateful acknowledgment of the kindness with which the series has thus far been received.

As in the case of the former plays, the text is the result of a careful collation of the Folio of 1623 with all the modern editions that have any critical value. With very few exceptions, the variations from the Folio, however trivial, have been mentioned in the notes, together with the readings adopted or proposed by the leading commentators. These textual questions are of interest to every student of Shakespeare, and my experience as a teacher has satisfied me that they may be profitably discussed even by boys and girls at school. Indeed, it sometimes happens that these babes in criticism are quick to see what is hidden from men reputed "wise and prudent." Their young eyes discern the simple truth through all the dust that successive generations of learned editors have raised in their quarrels about it.

In the Notes I have often referred the reader to illustrations of Shakespeare's English in the earlier books of the series, and the space thus gained has been used for *historical* annotations. The material for these has been drawn from a great variety of sources, and has been very carefully worked up. There are, of course, many notes which many of my readers will not need, but I think there are none that may not be of service, or at least of interest, to some of them.

Cambridge, Nov. 16, 1871.

CONTENTS.

	Page
Introduction to King Henry the Eighth	7
I. The History of the Play	7
II. The Historical Sources of the Play	14
III. Critical Comments on the Play	16
KING HENRY THE EIGHTH	43
Act I	47
" II	71
" III	95
" IV	118
" V	131
Notes	155

THE GLOBE THEATRE.

KING HENRY VIII.

INTRODUCTION

TO

KING HENRY THE EIGHTH.

I. THE HISTORY OF THE PLAY.

THIS drama, under the title of "The Famous History of the Life of King Henry the Eight," was first published in the Folio of 1623, where it occupies pages 205–232 in the division of "Histories." It is printed with remarkable accuracy, and the doubtful or disputed readings are comparatively few.

The date of the play has been the subject of much discussion. The earlier editors and commentators, with the single exception of Chalmers, believed that it was written before the death of Elizabeth (March, 1603), and that the allusion to her successor, "Nor shall this peace sleep with her," etc. (v. 4), did not form a part of Cranmer's speech as originally composed, but was interpolated by Ben Jonson after James had come to the throne. But, as White remarks, "the speech in question is homogeneous and Shakespearian; the subsequent allusion to Elizabeth as 'an aged princess' would not have been ventured during her life; and the exhibition of Henry's selfish passion for Anne Bullen, and of her lightness of character, would have been hardly less offensive to the Virgin Queen, her daughter." Knight, Collier, Dyce, Hudson, and other recent editors, take the same view.

But how early in the reign of James was the play written?

In the Stationers' Registers, under the date of February 12th, 1604[-5], we find the following memorandum:—"Nath. Butter] Yf he get good allowance for the Enterlude of K. Henry 8th before he begyn to print it, and then procure the wardens hands to yt for the entrance of yt, he is to have the same for his copy;" and Collier "feels no hesitation in concluding that it referred to Shakespeare's drama, which had probably been brought out at the Globe Theatre in the summer of 1604." Dyce is inclined to agree with Collier; but it is probable that Chalmers was right in assuming that the reference is to a play of Samuel Rowley's, "When you See me you Know me, or the Famous Chronicle History of King Henry the Eighth," which was published in 1605.

Knight, White, and Hudson believe that the play was written at Stratford in 1612 or 1613, and that it was the poet's last work. The weight of evidence, both external and internal, seems to me to be in favor of this opinion.

The Globe Theatre was burned down on the 29th* of June, 1613, and we have accounts of the accident from several witnesses. In Winwood's "Memorials" there is a letter from John Chamberlain to Sir Ralph Winwood, dated July 12th, 1613, which describes the burning, and says that it "fell out by a peale of chambers"—that is, a discharge of small cannon. In the Harleian Manuscripts we find a letter from Thomas Lorkin to Sir Thomas Puckering, dated "this last of June, 1613," which says, "No longer since than yesterday, while Bourbege his companie were acting at y^{e} Globe the play of Hen=8, and there shooting of certayne chambers in way of triumph, the fire catch'd." Sir Henry Wotton, writing to his nephew on the 6th of July, 1613, gives a minute account of the accident: "Now to let matters of state sleep, I will entertain you at the present with what happened this week at the Bankside. The king's players had *a new play* called *All is True*,† representing some *principal pieces of the reign of Henry the Eighth*, which was set forth with many extraordinary circumstances of pomp and majesty. . . . Now, King Henry making a mask at the Cardinal Wolsey's house, and certain cannons being shot off at his entry, some of the paper, or other stuff wherewith one of them was stopped, did light on the thatch, where, being thought at first but an idle smoke, and their eyes being more attentive to the show, it kindled inwardly, and ran round like a train, consuming, in less than an hour, the whole house to the very ground.

* White says "the 26th," but it is probably a slip of the type. Cf. Lorkin's letter, quoted below.

† A ballad of the time, entitled "The Lamentable Burning of the Globe Play-House on S. Peter's Day," has for the burden at the end of each stanza,

"O sorrow, pitiful sorrow!
And yet it All is True!"

In the fifth stanza we have the lines,

"Away ran Lady Katherine,
Nor waited for her trial,"

which prove that the trial of the Queen formed a part of the play.

This was the fatal period of that virtuous fabric, wherein yet nothing did perish but wood and straw, and a few forsaken cloaks; only one man had his breeches set on fire, that would perhaps have broiled him if he had not, by the benefit of a provident wit, put it out with bottle ale." Howes, in his continuation of Stowe's "Annales," written some time after the fire (since he speaks of the theatre as rebuilt "the next spring"), says that the house was "filled with people to behold the play, viz., of *Henry the Eighth.*" There can be little doubt that the play in question was Shakespeare's *Henry VIII.*, in which, according to the original stage direction (iv. 1), we have "chambers discharged" at the entrance of the king to the "mask at the cardinal's house." It appears to have had at first a double title, but the "All is True" was soon dropped, leaving only the more distinctive title corresponding to those of Shakespeare's other historical plays. There seem to be several references to the lost title in the Prologue: "May here find *truth* too;" "To rank our chosen *truth* with such a show;" and "To make that only *true* we now intend."

The evidence drawn from the play itself tends to confirm this view of its date. In the prophecy of Cranmer, the lines,

> "Wherever the bright sun of heaven shall shine,
> His honor, and the greatness of his name,
> Shall be, and make new nations,"

allude, we can hardly doubt, to the colonization of Virginia, and, if so, could not have been written earlier than 1607.

The style and the versification of the play, moreover, indicate that it was one of the last productions of the poet. As White has remarked, "the excessively elliptical construction, and the incessant use of verbal contractions, are marks of Shakespeare's latest years—those which produced *The Tempest* and *The Winter's Tale.*" It will be observed also that many of the lines end with unaccented monosyllables or particles; and Craik* has shown that this peculiarity is very rare in those plays of Shakespeare which are known to be his earliest, while it is frequent in those which are known to be his latest. "It was certainly a habit of writing which grew upon him after he once gave in to it."

Some critics have attempted to prove that portions of *Henry VIII.* were written by Fletcher, and others have maintained that Ben Jonson had a hand in its composition or its revision. Mr. Roderick, in notes appended to Edwards's "Canons of Criticism," was the first to point out certain peculiarities in the versification of the play—the frequent occurrence of a redundant or eleventh syllable, of pauses nearer the end of the verse than usual, and of "emphasis clashing with the cadence of the metre." Mr. Spedding (*Gentleman's Magazine,* Aug., 1851) and Mr. Hickson (*Notes and Queries,* vol. ii., p. 198, and vol. iii., p. 33) both fix on certain scenes as Fletcher's, basing their opinion on the structure of the verse, and the recurrence of words and phrases which they think peculiar to Fletcher. Craik (*English of Shakespeare,* Rolfe's ed., pp. 10, 38) believes that much of the play is "evidently by another hand," the character of the versification being "the most conclusive, or, at least, the clearest evidence that it can not have been written throughout by Shakespeare." Abbott (*Shakespearian Grammar,* p. 331), after stating that in Shakespeare's verse "the extra syllable [at the end of a line] is very rarely a monosyllable," says: "The fact that in *Henry VIII.*, and in no other play of Shakespeare's, *constant exceptions are found to this rule,* seems to me a sufficient proof that Shakespeare did not write that play."

On the other hand, Mr. Courtenay (*Comments on the Historical Plays,* vol. ii., p. 172), referring to Roderick's criticisms, says: "How Shakespeare came thus to vary his measure I can not guess, but that it is *his* measure I see not the least reason for doubting. I know that even in prose the con-

* See his "English of Shakespeare" (Rolfe's ed.), pp. 35–42.

struction of sentences, and (if I may say so) *the air*, is much affected by the tone of the writer's mind at the moment, and by the nature of the subject." The notion of the clashing of the emphasis with the metre "gives too much importance to *quantity*, which scarcely prevails in English;" and, besides, the assertion that there is such clashing does not appear to be well founded. Singer, in his Introduction to the play, remarks: "I must confess that I have no faith in the deductions from the structure of the verse; Shakespeare is so varied in this respect that, upon the same ground, other portions of his works might be brought in question. The peculiarities of language, too, are pretty uniformly distributed, and some of them will be found in those scenes which Spedding and Hickson have given to Shakespeare." Knight (Supplementary Notice, in his *Pictorial Edition*) admits that there are peculiarities in the verse "not found in any other of Shakespeare's works;" but holds, nevertheless, that the theory of its not being wholly his own is "utterly untenable." He adds: "There is no play of Shakespeare's which has a more decided character of unity—no one from which any passage could be less easily struck out. We believe that Shakespeare worked in this particular upon a principle of art which he had proposed to himself to adhere to, wherever the nature of the scene would allow. The elliptical construction, and the license of versification, brought the dialogue, whenever the speaker was not necessarily rhetorical, closer to the language of common life. Of all his historical plays, the *Henry VIII.* is the nearest in its story to his own times. It professed to be a 'truth.' It belongs to his own country. It has no poetical indistinctness about it, either of time or place; all is defined. If the diction and the versification had been more artificial, it would have been less a reality."

The leading German critics differ no less widely in their views. Gervinus (*Shakespeare Commentaries*) thinks that

Shakespeare prepared a mere sketch of the play, and gave it to Fletcher to be finished. The former was the only poet of the time who could have "sketched the psychological outlines of the main characters with so much sharpness;" but "Fletcher's rhythmic manner is strikingly conspicuous throughout." There is also a "lack of dramatic unity," and a "looseness in the development of the action," which show that the outline from the hand of the great master was filled out by an inferior artist.

Ulrici, on the other hand, in his *Shakespeare's Dramatic Art*, maintains that "all the internal marks of style, language, character, and versification" prove that the play is Shakespeare's. He thinks it not improbable that it was written in honor of the nuptials of the Palsgrave Frederick and the Princess Elizabeth in 1613. "It is certain that during the Palsgrave's visit several of Shakespeare's plays were performed before the court, and among them *The Tempest*, which contains many palpable allusions to the marriage festival." The peculiarities of style and versification are to be explained by assuming "either that Shakespeare was hurried by the sudden command of the court to produce a new drama for the nuptial festivities, or probably merely by the event itself, or that he composed the play in the last years of his life, and consequently had no time for a careful revision of it."

For myself, I have no hesitation in accepting the play as Shakespeare's. He may not have written the Prologue and Epilogue—a point which will be more fully discussed in the Notes; but, as Gervinus has said, no other poet of the time could have drawn the outlines of the leading characters of the drama, and even the details of the picture show the hand of a greater than Fletcher or Jonson. The peculiarities of style and measure may be explained either as Knight or as Ulrici has suggested; but, even if we admit that they are inexplicable, they are of small account in comparison with these "weightier matters" of internal evidence.

WOLSEY'S HALL.

II. THE HISTORICAL SOURCES OF THE PLAY.

The historical authorities followed by Shakespeare in the first four acts of the play were Edward Hall's "Union of the

Families of Lancaster and York," the first edition of which appeared in 1548, and Raphael Holinshed's "Chronicles of England, Scotland, and Ireland," published in 1577. These writers had copied largely from George Cavendish's "Life of Cardinal Wolsey," of which there were many manuscript copies in Shakespeare's day, though the work was not printed until 1641. For the fifth act he took his materials from John Fox's "Acts and Monuments of the Church," published in 1563.

In these books the poet found many details which he has put into dramatic form with very slight change of language, as will be seen from the illustrations given in our Notes. The action of the play includes events scattered through a period of about twenty-three years, or from 1520 to 1543, and the events are not always given in their chronological order. Thus the reversal of the decree for taxing the commons (1525) and the examination of Buckingham's surveyor (1521) are in one scene; the banquet scene (1526) precedes that of Buckingham's execution, and in the latter scene we find mention of Henry's scruples concerning his marriage (1527) and of the arrival of Campeggio (1529); the scene in which Anne is made Marchioness of Pembroke (1532) precedes that of the trial of the queen (1529); the death of Wolsey (1530) is announced to Katherine in the scene in which she dies (1536); in the same scene in which the birth of Elizabeth (1533) is announced to the king, he converses with Cranmer about the charge of heresy (1543); and in the scene in which Cranmer is accused before the council (1543), Henry asks him to be godfather at the baptism of Elizabeth (1533). Even if we make no account of the introduction of the charges against Cranmer (1543), the action of the play will cover a period of some sixteen years, from the return of the English Court from the Field of the Cloth of Gold in 1520, to the death of Katherine in 1536.

QUEEN KATHERINE.

III. CRITICAL COMMENTS ON THE PLAY.

[*From Mrs. Jameson's "Characteristics of Women."*]

QUEEN KATHERINE OF ARRAGON.*

To have a just idea of the accuracy and beauty of this historical portrait, we ought to bring immediately before us those circumstances of Katherine's life and times, and those parts of her character, which belong to a period previous to the opening of the play. We shall then be better able to appreciate the skill with which Shakespeare has applied the materials before him.

* I know of no better Historical Introduction to the play than this admirable paper, which I therefore give almost entire—omitting merely a paragraph devoted to a comparison of the characters of Katherine and of Hermione in *The Winter's Tale*.

Katherine of Arragon, the fourth and youngest daughter of Ferdinand, king of Arragon, and Isabella of Castile, was born at Alcala, whither her mother had retired to winter after one of the most terrible campaigns of the Moorish war—that of 1485.

Katherine had derived from nature no dazzling qualities of mind, and no striking advantages of person. She inherited a tincture of Queen Isabella's haughtiness and obstinacy of temper, but neither her beauty nor her splendid talents. Her education, under the direction of her extraordinary mother, had implanted in her mind the most austere principles of virtue, the highest ideas of female decorum, the most narrow and bigoted attachment to the forms of religion, and that excessive pride of birth and rank which distinguished so particularly her family and her nation. In other respects, her understanding was strong and her judgment clear. The natural turn of her mind was simple, serious, and domestic, and all the impulses of her heart kindly and benevolent. Such was Katherine; such, at least, she appears on a reference to the chronicles of her times, and particularly from her own letters, and the papers written or dictated by herself which relate to her divorce; all of which are distinguished by the same artless simplicity of style, the same quiet good sense, the same resolute yet gentle spirit and fervent piety.

When five years old, Katherine was solemnly affianced to Arthur, prince of Wales, the eldest son of Henry VII.; and in the year 1501 she landed in England, after narrowly escaping shipwreck on the southern coast, from which every adverse wind conspired to drive her. She was received in London with great honour, and immediately on her arrival united to the young prince. He was then fifteen, and Katherine in her seventeenth year.

Arthur, as it is well known, survived his marriage only five months; and the reluctance of Henry VII. to refund the splendid dowry of the Infanta, and forego the advantages of an alliance with the most powerful prince of Europe, suggested the idea of uniting Katherine to his second son Henry; after some hesitation a dispensation was procured from the pope, and she was betrothed to Henry in her eighteenth year. The prince, who was then only twelve years old, resisted as far as he was able to do so, and appears to have really felt a degree of horror at the idea of marrying his brother's widow. Nor was the mind of King Henry at rest; as his health declined, his conscience reproached him with the equivocal nature of the union into which he had forced his son, and the vile motives of avarice and expediency which had governed him on this occasion. A short time previous to his death he dissolved the engagement, and even caused Henry to sign a paper in which he solemnly renounced all idea of a future union with the Infanta. It is observable that Henry signed this paper with reluctance, and that Katherine, instead of being sent back to her own country, still remained in England.

It appears that Henry, who was now about seventeen, had become interested for Katherine, who was gentle and amiable. The difference of years was rather a circumstance in her favor; for Henry was just at that age when a youth is most likely to be captivated by a woman older than himself: and no sooner was he required to renounce her than the interest she had gradually gained in his affections became, by opposition, a strong passion. Immediately after his father's death he declared his resolution to take for his wife the Lady Katherine of Spain, and none other; and when the matter was discussed in council, it was urged that, besides the many advantages of the match in a political point of view, she had given so "much proof of virtue and sweetness of condition as they knew not where to parallel her." About six weeks after his accession, June 3, 1509, the marriage was celebrated with truly royal splendour, Henry being then eighteen and Katherine in her twenty-fourth year.

It has been said with truth, that if Henry had died while Katherine was yet his wife and Wolsey his minister, he would have left behind him the character of a magnificent, popular, and accomplished prince, instead of that of the most hateful ruffian and tyrant who ever swayed these realms. Notwithstanding his occasional infidelities, and his impatience at her midnight vigils, her long prayers, and her religious austerities, Katherine and Henry lived in harmony together. He was fond of openly displaying his respect and love for her, and she exercised a strong and salutary influence over his turbulent and despotic spirit. When Henry set out on his expedition to France in 1513, he left Katherine regent of the kingdom during his absence, with full powers to carry on the war against the Scots, and the Earl of Surrey at the head of the army as her lieutenant general. It is curious to find Katherine—the pacific, domestic, and unpretending Katherine—describing herself as having "her heart set to war," and "horrible busy" with making "standards, banners, badges, scarfs, and the like."* Nor was this mere silken preparation—mere dalliance with the pomp and circumstance of war; for within a few weeks afterward her general defeated the Scots in the famous battle of Floddenfield, where James IV. and most of his nobility were slain.†

Katherine's letter to Henry, announcing this event, so strikingly displays the piety and tenderness, the quiet simplicity, and real magnanimity of her character, that there can not be a more apt and beautiful illustration of the exquisite truth and keeping of Shakespeare's portrait.

SIR,—My Lord Howard hath sent me a letter, open to your Grace, within one of mine, by the which ye shall see at

* See her letters in Ellis's Collection.

† Under similar circumstances, one of Katherine's predecessors, Philippa of Hainault, had gained in her husband's absence the battle of Neville Cross, in which David Bruce was taken prisoner.

length the great victory that our Lord hath sent your subjects in your absence: and for this cause it is no need herein to trouble your Grace with long writing; but to my thinking this battle hath been to your Grace, and all your realm, the greatest honour that could be, and more than ye should win all the crown of France, thanked be God for it! And I am sure your Grace forgetteth not to do this, which shall be cause to send you many more such great victories, as I trust he shall do. My husband, for haste, with Rougecross, I could not send your Grace the piece of the King of Scots' coat, which John Glyn now bringeth. In this your Grace shall see how I can keep my promise, sending you for your banners a king's coat. I thought to send himself unto you, but our Englishmen's hearts would not suffer it. It should have been better for him to have been in peace than have this reward, but all that God sendeth is for the best. My Lord of Surrey, my Henry, would fain know your pleasure in the burying of the King of Scots' body, for he hath written to me so. With the next messenger your Grace's pleasure may be herein known. And with this I make an end, praying God to send you home shortly; for without this no joy here can be accomplished—and for the same I pray. And now go to our Lady at Walsyngham, that I promised so long ago to see.

At Woburn, the 16th day of September (1513).

I send your Grace herein a bill, found in a Scottishman's purse, of such things as the French king sent to the said King of Scots, to make war against you, beseeching you to send Mathew hither as soon as this messenger cometh with tidings of your Grace. Your humble wife and true servant,

KATHERINE.*

* Ellis's Collection. We must keep in mind that Katherine was a foreigner, and till after she was seventeen never spoke or wrote a word of English.

The legality of the king's marriage with Katherine remained undisputed till 1527. In the course of that year Anna Bullen first appeared at court, and was appointed maid of honor to the queen; and then, and not till then, did Henry's union with his brother's wife "creep too near his conscience." In the following year he sent special messengers to Rome with secret instructions: they were required to discover (among other "hard questions") whether, if the queen entered a religious life, the king might have the pope's dispensation to marry again; and whether, if the king (for the better inducing the queen thereto) would enter himself into a religious life, the pope would dispense with the king's vow, and leave her there?

Poor Katherine! we are not surprised to read that when she understood what was intended against her, "she labored with all those passions which jealousy of the king's affection, sense of her own honour, and the legitimation of her daughter could produce, laying in conclusion the whole fault on the cardinal." (It is elsewhere said that Wolsey bore the queen ill-will in consequence of her reflecting with some severity on his haughty temper and very unclerical life.

The proceedings were pending for nearly six years, and one of the causes of this long delay, in spite of Henry's impatient and despotic character, is worth noting. The old Chronicle tells us that, though the men generally, and more particularly the priests and the nobles, sided with Henry in this matter, yet all the ladies of England were against it. They justly felt that the honour and welfare of no woman was secure if, after twenty years of union, she might be thus deprived of all her rights as a wife; the clamour became so loud and general that the king was obliged to yield to it for a time, to stop the proceedings, and to banish Anna Bullen from the court.

Cardinal Campeggio, called by Shakespeare Campeius, arrived in England in October, 1528. He at first endeavoured to persuade Katherine to avoid the disgrace and danger of contesting her marriage by entering a religious house; but she rejected his advice with strong expressions of disdain. "I am," said she, "the king's true wife, and to him married; and if all doctors were dead, or law or learning far out of men's minds at the time of our marriage, yet I cannot think that the court of Rome, and the whole Church of England, would have consented to a thing unlawful and detestable as you call it. Still I say I am his wife, and for him will I pray."

About two years afterwards Wolsey died (in November, 1530)—the king and queen met for the last time on the 14th of July, 1531. Until that period, some outward show of respect and kindness had been maintained between them; but the king then ordered her to repair to a private residence, and no longer to consider herself as his lawful wife. "To which the virtuous and mourning queen replied no more than this, that to whatever place she removed, nothing could remove her from being the king's wife. And so they bid each other farewell; and from this time the king never saw her more."* He married Anna Bullen in 1532, while the decision relating to his former marriage was still pending. The sentence of divorce, to which Katherine never would submit, was finally pronounced by Cranmer in 1533; and the unhappy queen, whose health had been gradually declining through these troubles of heart, died January 29, 1536, in the fiftieth year of her age.

Thus the action of the play of Henry VIII. includes events which occurred from the impeachment of the Duke of Buckingham in 1521, to the death of Katherine in 1536. In making the death of Katherine precede the birth of Queen Elizabeth, Shakespeare has committed an anachronism, not only pardonable, but necessary. We must remember that the construction of the play required a happy termination; and that the birth of Elizabeth, before or after the death of Kath-

* Hall's Chronicle.

erine, involved the question of her legitimacy. By this slight deviation from the real course of events, Shakespeare has not perverted historic facts, but merely sacrificed them to a higher principle; and in doing so has not only preserved dramatic propriety, and heightened the poetical interest, but has given a strong proof both of his delicacy and his judgment.

If we also call to mind that in this play Katherine is properly the heroine, and exhibited from first to last as the very "queen of earthly queens;" that the whole interest is thrown round her and Wolsey—the one the injured rival, the other the enemy of Anna Bullen—and that it was written in the reign and for the court of Elizabeth, we shall yet farther appreciate the moral greatness of the poet's mind, which disdained to sacrifice justice and the truth of nature to any time-serving expediency.

Schlegel observes somewhere, that in the literal accuracy and apparent artlessness with which Shakespeare has adapted some of the events and characters of history to his dramatic purposes, he has shown equally his genius and his wisdom. This, like most of Schlegel's remarks, is profound and true; and in this respect Katherine of Arragon may rank as the triumph of Shakespeare's genius and his wisdom. There is nothing in the whole range of poetical fiction in any respect resembling or approaching her; there is nothing comparable, I suppose, but Katherine's own portrait by Holbein, which, equally true to the life, is yet as far inferior as Katherine's person was inferior to her mind. Not only has Shakespeare given us here a delineation as faithful as it is beautiful, of a peculiar modification of character, but he has bequeathed us a precious moral lesson in this proof that virtue alone—(by which I mean here the union of truth or conscience with benevolent affection—the one the highest law, the other the purest impulse of the soul)—that such virtue is a sufficient source of the deepest pathos and power without any mixture of foreign or external ornament: for who but Shakespeare would have brought before us a queen and a heroine of tragedy, stripped her of all pomp of place and circumstance, dispensed with all the usual sources of poetical interest, as youth, beauty, grace, fancy, commanding intellect, and without any appeal to our imagination, without any violation of historical truth, or any sacrifices of the other dramatic personages for the sake of effect, could depend on the moral principle alone to touch the very springs of feeling in our bosoms, and melt and elevate our hearts through the purest and holiest impulses of our nature!

The character, when analyzed, is, in the first place, distinguished by *truth*. I do not only mean its truth to nature, or its relative truth arising from its historic fidelity and dramatic consistency, but *truth* as a quality of the soul: this is the basis of the character. We often hear it remarked that those who are themselves perfectly true and artless are in this world the more easily and frequently deceived—a commonplace fallacy: for we shall ever find that truth is as undeceived as it is undeceiving, and that those who are true to themselves and others may now and then be mistaken, or in particular instances duped by the intervention of some other affection or quality of the mind; but they are generally free from illusion, and they are seldom imposed upon in the long run by the shows of things and superfices of characters. It is by this integrity of heart and clearness of understanding, this light of truth within her own soul, and not through any acuteness of intellect, that Katherine detects and exposes the real character of Wolsey, though unable either to unravel his designs or defeat them.

> . . . . My lord, my lord,
> I am a simple woman, much too weak
> T' oppose your cunning.

She rather intuitively feels than knows his duplicity, and in the dignity of her simplicity she towers above his arrogance as much as she scorns his crooked policy. With this essential truth are combined many other qualities, natural or acquired, all made out with the same uncompromising breadth of execution and fidelity of pencil, united with the utmost delicacy of feeling. For instance, the apparent contradiction arising from the contrast between Katherine's natural disposition and the situation in which she is placed; her lofty Castilian pride and her extreme simplicity of language and deportment; the inflexible resolution with which she asserts her right, and her soft resignation to unkindness and wrong; her warmth of temper breaking through the meekness of a spirit subdued by a deep sense of religion; and a degree of austerity tinging her real benevolence—all these qualities, opposed yet harmonizing, has Shakespeare placed before us in a few admirable scenes.

Katherine is at first introduced as pleading before the king in behalf of the commonalty, who had been driven by the extortions of Wolsey into some illegal excesses. In this scene, which is true to history, we have her upright reasoning mind, her steadiness of purpose, her piety and benevolence, placed in a strong light. The unshrinking dignity with which she opposes without descending to brave the cardinal, the stern rebuke addressed to the Duke of Buckingham's surveyor, are finely characteristic; and by thus exhibiting Katherine as invested with all her conjugal rights and influence, and royal state, the subsequent situations are rendered more impressive. She is placed in the first instance on such a height in our esteem and reverence, that in the midst of her abandonment and degradation, and the profound pity she afterwards inspires, the first effect remains unimpaired, and she never falls beneath it.

In the beginning of the second act we are prepared for the proceedings of the divorce, and our respect for Katherine heightened by the general sympathy for "the good queen," as she is expressively entitled, and by the following beautiful eulogium on her character uttered by the Duke of Norfolk:—

He (Wolsey) counsels a divorce : a loss of her
That like a jewel has hung twenty years
About his neck, yet never lost her lustre.
Of her that loves him with that excellence
That angels love good men with ; even of her,
That when the greatest stroke of fortune falls,
Will bless the king !

The scene in which Anna Bullen is introduced as expressing her grief and sympathy for her royal mistress is exquisitely graceful.

Here's the pang that pinches :
His highness having liv'd so long with her, and she
So good a lady, that no tongue could ever
Pronounce dishonour of her,—by my life
She never knew harm-doing ;—O now, after
So many courses of the sun enthron'd,
Still growing in a majesty and pomp, the which
To leave, a thousand fold more bitter than
'Tis sweet at first t' acquire,—after this process,
To give her the avaunt ! it is a pity
Would move a monster.
Old Lady. Hearts of most hard temper
Melt and lament for her.
Anne. O, God's will ! much better
She ne'er had known pomp : though it be temporal,
Yet if that quarrel, Fortune, do divorce
It from the bearer, 'tis a sufferance panging
As soul and body's severing.
Old Lady. Alas, poor lady !
She's a stranger now again.
Anne. So much the more
Must pity drop upon her. Verily,
I swear 'tis better to be lowly born,
And range with humble livers in content,
Than to be perk'd up in a glistering grief,
And wear a golden sorrow.

How completely, in the few passages appropriated to Anna Bullen, is her character portrayed ? with what a delicate and yet luxuriant grace is she sketched off, with her gayety and her beauty, her levity, her extreme mobility, her sweetness of disposition, her tenderness of heart, and, in short, all her *femalities!* How nobly has Shakespeare done justice to the two women, and heightened our interest in both by placing the praises of Katherine in the mouth of Anna Bullen! and how characteristic of the latter, that she should first express unbounded pity for her mistress, insisting chiefly on her fall from her regal state and worldly pomp, thus betraying her own disposition:—

> For she that had all the fair parts of woman,
> Had, too, a woman's heart, which ever yet
> Affected eminence, wealth, sovereignty.

That she should call the loss of temporal pomp, once enjoyed, "a sufferance equal to soul and body's severing;" that she should immediately protest that she would not herself be a queen—"No, good troth! not for all the riches under heaven!"—and not long afterwards ascend without reluctance that throne and bed from which her royal mistress had been so cruelly divorced!—how natural! The portrait is not less true and masterly than that of Katherine; but the character is overborne by the superior moral firmness and intrinsic excellence of the latter. That we may be more fully sensible of this contrast, the beautiful scene just alluded to immediately precedes Katherine's trial at Blackfriars, and the description of Anna Bullen's triumphant beauty at her coronation is placed immediately before the dying scene of Katherine; yet with equal good taste and good feeling Shakespeare has constantly avoided all personal collision between the two characters; nor does Anna Bullen ever appear as queen except in the pageant of the procession, which in reading the play is scarcely noticed.

To return to Katherine. The whole of the trial scene is given nearly verbatim from the old chronicles and records; but the dryness and harshness of the law proceedings is tempered at once and elevated by the genius and the wisdom of the poet. It appears, on referring to the historical authorities, that when the affair was first agitated in council, Katherine replied to the long expositions and theological sophistries of her opponents with resolute simplicity and composure: "I am a woman, and lack wit and learning to answer these opinions; but I am sure that neither the king's father nor my father would have condescended to our marriage if it had been judged unlawful. As to your saying that I should put the cause to eight persons of this realm, for quietness of the king's conscience, I pray Heaven to send his grace a quiet conscience; and this shall be your answer, that I say I am his lawful wife, and to him lawfully married, though not worthy of it; and in this point I will abide, till the court of Rome, which was privy to the beginning, have made a final ending of it."*

Katherine's appearance in the court at Blackfriars, attended by a noble troop of ladies and prelates of her counsel, and her refusal to answer the citation, are historical.† Her speech to the king—

> Sir, I desire you do me right and justice,
> And to bestow your pity on me, etc.—

is taken word for word (as nearly as the change from prose to blank verse would allow) from the old record in Hall. It would have been easy for Shakespeare to have exalted his own skill by throwing a colouring of poetry and eloquence into this speech, without altering the sense or sentiment; but by adhering to the calm argumentative simplicity of manner and diction natural to the woman, he has preserved the truth

* Hall's Chronicle, p. 781.

† The court at Blackfriars sat on the 28th of May, 1529. "The queen being called, accompanied by the four bishops and others of her counsel, and a great company of ladies and gentlewomen following her; and after her obeisance, sadly and with great gravity, she appealed from them to the court of Rome."—*See Hall and Cavendish's Life of Wolsey.*

The account which Hume gives of this scene is very elegant; but after the affecting *naïveté* of the old chroniclers, it is very cold and unsatisfactory.

of character without lessening the pathos of the situation. Her challenging Wolsey as a "foe to truth," and her very expressions, "I utterly refuse,—yea, from my soul *abhor* you for my judge," are taken from fact. The sudden burst of indignant passion towards the close of this scene,

In one who ever yet
Had stood to charity, and displayed the effects
Of disposition gentle, and of wisdom
O'ertopping woman's power;

is taken from nature, though it occurred on a different occasion.*

Lastly, the circumstance of her being called back after she had appealed from the court, and angrily refusing to return, is from the life. Master Griffith, on whose arm she leaned, observed that she was called: "On, on," quoth she; "it maketh no matter, for it is no indifferent court for me, therefore I will not tarry. Go on your ways."†

King Henry's own assertion, "I dare to say, my lords, that for her womanhood, wisdom, nobility, and gentleness, never prince had such another wife, and therefore if I would willingly change her I were not wise," is thus beautifully paraphrased by Shakespeare:—

That man i' th' world, who shall report he has
A better wife, let him in naught be trusted,
For speaking false in that! Thou art, alone
(If thy rare qualities, sweet gentleness,
Thy meekness saint-like, wife-like government,
Obeying in commanding, and thy parts,
Sovereign and pious else, could speak thee out),
The queen of earthly queens.—She's noble born;
And, like her true nobility, she has
Carried herself towards me.

---

* "The queen answered the Duke of Suffolk very highly and obstinately, with many high words: and suddenly, in a fury, she departed from him into her privy chamber."—*Vide Hall's Chronicle.*

† *Vide* Cavendish's Life of Wolsey.

We are told by Cavendish, that when Wolsey and Campeggio visited the queen by the king's order she was found at work among her women, and came forth to meet the cardinals with a skein of white thread hanging about her neck; that when Wolsey addressed her in Latin, she interrupted him, saying, "Nay, good my lord, speak to me in English, I beseech you; although I understand Latin." "Forsooth then," quoth my lord, "madam, if it please your grace, we come both to know your mind, how ye be disposed to do in this matter between the king and you, and also to declare secretly our opinions and our counsel unto you, which we have intended of very zeal and obedience that we bear to your grace." "My lords, I thank you then," quoth she, "of your good wills; but to make answer to your request I cannot so suddenly, for I was set among my maidens at work, thinking full little of any such matter; wherein there needeth a longer deliberation, and a better head than mine to make answer to so noble wise men as ye be. I had need of good counsel in this case, which toucheth me so near; and for any counsel or friendship that I can find in England, they are nothing to my purpose or profit. Think you, I pray you, my lords, will any Englishmen counsel, or be friendly unto me, against the king's pleasure, they being his subjects? Nay, forsooth, my lords! and for my counsel, in whom I do intend to put my trust, they be not here; they be in Spain, in my native country.* Alas! my lords, I am a poor woman lacking both wit and understanding sufficiently to answer such approved wise men as ye be both, in so weighty a matter. I pray you to extend your good and indifferent minds in your authority unto me, for I

* This affecting passage is thus rendered by Shakespeare (iii. 1.):—

> Nay, forsooth, my friends,
> They that must weigh out my afflictions,
> They that my trust must grow to, live not here:
> They are, as all my other comforts, far hence,
> In mine own country, lords.

am a simple woman, destitute and barren of friendship and counsel, here in a foreign region; and as for your counsel, I will not refuse, but be glad to hear."

It appears, also, that when the Archbishop of York and Bishop Tunstall waited on her at her house near Huntingdon, with the sentence of the divorce, signed by Henry, and confirmed by an act of Parliament, she refused to admit its validity, she being Henry's wife, and not his subject. The bishop describes her conduct in his letter: "She being therewith in great choler and agony, and always interrupting our words, declared that she would never leave the name of queen, but would persist in accounting herself the king's wife till death." When the official letter containing minutes of their conference was shown to her, she seized a pen and dashed it angrily across every sentence in which she was styled *Princess-dowager.*

If now we turn to that inimitable scene between Katherine and the two cardinals (act iii. scene 1), we shall observe how finely Shakespeare has condensed these incidents, and unfolded to us all the workings of Katherine's proud yet feminine nature. She is discovered at work with some of her women—she calls for music "to soothe her soul grown sad with troubles"—then follows the little song, of which the sentiment is so well adapted to the occasion, while its quaint yet classic elegance breathes the very spirit of those times when Surrey loved and sung. They are interrupted by the arrival of the two cardinals. Katherine's perception of their subtlety—her suspicion of their purpose—her sense of her own weakness and inability to contend with them, and her mild subdued dignity, are beautifully represented; as also the guarded self-command with which she eludes giving a definitive answer; but when they counsel her to that which she, who knows Henry, feels must end in her ruin, then the native temper is roused at once, or, to use Tunstall's expression, "the choler and the agony," burst forth in words.

Is this your Christian counsel? Out upon ye!
Heaven is above all yet; there sits a Judge
That no king can corrupt.
Wolsey. Your rage mistakes us.
Queen Katherine. The more shame for ye! Holy men I thought ye,
Upon my soul, two reverend cardinal virtues;
But cardinal sins, and hollow hearts, I fear ye:
Mend 'em, for shame, my lords. Is this your comfort,
The cordial that ye bring a wretched lady?

With the same force of language, and impetuous yet dignified feeling, she asserts her own conjugal truth and merit, and insists upon her rights.

Have I liv'd thus long (let me speak myself,
Since virtue finds no friends), a wife, a true one
A woman (I dare say, without vain-glory)
Never yet branded with suspicion?
Have I with all my full affections
Still met the king? lov'd him next heaven? obey'd him?
Been, out of fondness, superstitious to him?
Almost forgot my prayers to content him?
And am I thus rewarded? 'tis not well, lords, etc.

My lord, I dare not make myself so guilty,
To give up willingly that noble title
Your master wed me to: nothing but death
Shall e'er divorce my dignities.

And this burst of unwonted passion is immediately followed by the natural reaction; it subsides into tears, dejection, and a mournful self-compassion.

Would I had never trod this English ground,
Or felt the flatteries that grow upon it!
What will become of me now, wretched lady?
I am the most unhappy woman living.—
Alas, poor wenches, where are now your fortunes? [*To her women.*
Shipwracked upon a kingdom where no pity,
No friends, no hope, no kindred weep for me!
Almost no grave allowed me!—Like the lily,

> That once was mistress of the field, and flourish'd,
> I'll hang my head and perish.

Dr. Johnson observes on this scene that all Katherine's distresses could not save her from a quibble on the word *cardinal*:

> Holy men I thought ye,
> Upon my soul, two reverend cardinal virtues;
> But cardinal sins, and hollow hearts, I fear ye!

When we read this passage in connection with the situation and sentiment, the scornful play upon the words is not only appropriate and natural, it seems inevitable. Katherine, assuredly, is neither an imaginative nor a witty personage; but we all acknowledge the truism that anger inspires wit, and whenever there is passion there is poetry. In the instance just alluded to, the sarcasm springs naturally out from the bitter indignation of the moment. In her grand rebuke of Wolsey, in the trial scene, how just and beautiful is the gradual elevation of her language, till it rises into that magnificent image—

> You have by fortune and his highness' favours,
> Gone slightly o'er low steps, and now are mounted,
> Where powers are your retainers, etc.

In the depth of her affliction, the pathos as naturally clothes itself in poetry.

> Like the lily,
> That once was mistress of the field, and flourish'd,
> I'll hang my head and perish.

But these, I believe, are the only instances of imagery throughout; for, in general, her language is plain and energetic. It has the strength and simplicity of her character, with very little metaphor and less wit.

In approaching the last scene of Katherine's life, I feel as if about to tread within a sanctuary where nothing befits us but silence and tears; veneration so strives with compassion, tenderness with awe.*

* Dr. Johnson is of opinion that this scene "is above any other part of

We must suppose a long interval to have elapsed since Katherine's interview with the two cardinals. Wolsey was disgraced, and poor Anna Bullen at the height of her short-lived prosperity. It was Wolsey's fate to be detested by both queens. In the pursuance of his own selfish and ambitious designs, he had treated both with perfidy; and one was the remote, the other the immediate cause of his ruin.*

The ruffian king, of whom one hates to think, was bent on forcing Katherine to concede her rights, and illegitimize her daughter, in favor of the offspring of Anna Bullen: she steadily refused, was declared contumacious, and the sentence of divorce pronounced in 1533. Such of her attendants as persisted in paying her the honours due to a queen were driven from her household; those who consented to serve her as princess-dowager she refused to admit into her presence; so

Shakespeare's tragedies, and perhaps above any scene of any other poet, tender and pathetic; without gods, or furies, or poisons, or precipices; without the help of romantic circumstances; without improbable sallies of poetical lamentation, and without any throes of tumultuous misery."

I have already observed that, in judging of Shakespeare's characters as of persons we meet in real life, we are swayed unconsciously by our own habits and feelings, and our preference governed, more or less, by our individual prejudices or sympathies. Thus Dr. Johnson, who has not a word to bestow on Imogen, and who has treated poor Juliet as if she had been in truth "the very beadle to an amorous sigh," does full justice to the character of Katherine, because the logical turn of his mind, his vigorous intellect, and his austere integrity, enabled him to appreciate its peculiar beauties; and, accordingly, we find that he gives it, not only unqualified, but almost exclusive admiration: he goes so far as to assert that in this play the genius of Shakespeare comes in and goes out with Katherine.

* It will be remembered that in early youth Anna Bullen was betrothed to Lord Henry Percy, who was passionately in love with her. Wolsey, to serve the king's purposes, broke off this match, and forced Percy into an unwilling marriage with Lady Mary Talbot. "The stout Earl of Northumberland," who arrested Wolsey at York, was this very Percy: he was chosen for his mission by the interference of Anna Bullen—a piece of vengeance truly feminine in its mixture of sentiment and spitefulness, and every way characteristic of the individual woman.

that she remained unattended except by a few women, and her gentleman usher, Griffith. During the last eighteen months of her life she resided at Kimbolton. Her nephew, Charles V., had offered her an asylum and princely treatment; but Katherine, broken in heart and declining in health, was unwilling to drag the spectacle of her misery and degradation into a strange country: she pined in her loneliness, deprived of her daughter, receiving no consolation from the pope, and no redress from the emperor. Wounded pride, wronged affection, and a cankering jealousy of the woman preferred to her (which, though it never broke out into unseemly words, is enumerated as one of the causes of her death), at length wore out a feeble frame. "Thus," says the chronicle, "Queen Katherine fell into her last sickness; and though the king sent to comfort her through Chapuys, the emperor's ambassador, she grew worse and worse; and finding death now coming, she caused a maid attending on her to write to the king to this effect:—

"My most dear Lord, King, and Husband:—

"The hour of my death now approaching, I cannot choose but, out of the love I bear you, advise you of your soul's health, which you ought to prefer before all considerations of the world or flesh whatsoever; for which yet you have cast me into many calamities, and yourself into many troubles: but I forgive you all, and pray God to do so likewise; for the rest, I commend unto you Mary our daughter, beseeching you to be a good father to her, as I have heretofore desired. I must intreat you also to respect my maids, and give them in marriage, which is not much, they being but three, and all my other servants a year's pay besides their due, lest otherwise they be unprovided for: lastly, I make this vow, that mine eyes desire you above all things.—Farewell!"*

* The king is said to have wept on reading this letter, and her body being interred at Peterbro', in the monastery, for honour of her memory

She also wrote another letter to the ambassador, desiring that he would remind the king of her dying request, and urge him to do her this last right.

What the historian relates, Shakespeare realizes. On the wonderful beauty of Katherine's closing scene we need not dwell, for that requires no illustration. In transferring the sentiments of her letter to her lips, Shakespeare has given them added grace, and pathos, and tenderness, without injuring their truth and simplicity: the feelings, and almost the manner of expression, are Katherine's own. The severe justice with which she draws the character of Wolsey is extremely characteristic; the benign candour with which she listens to the praise of him "whom living she most hated," is not less so. How beautiful her religious enthusiasm!—the slumber which visits her pillow, as she listens to that sad music she called her knell; her awakening from the vision of celestial joy to find herself still on earth—

> Spirits of peace! where are ye? Are ye all gone,
> And leave me here in wretchedness behind ye?—

how unspeakably beautiful! And to consummate all in one final touch of truth and nature, we see that consciousness of her own worth and integrity which had sustained her through all her trials of heart, and that pride of station for which she had contended through long years,—which had become more dear by opposition, and by the perseverance with which she had asserted it,—remaining the last strong feeling upon her mind, to the very last hour of existence.

> When I am dead, good wench,
> Let me be used with honour: strew me over
> With maiden flowers, that all the world may know
> I was a chaste wife to my grave; embalm me,
> Then lay me forth: although unqueen'd, yet like
> A queen, and daughter to a king, inter me.
> I can no more.

---

it was preserved at the dissolution, and erected into a bishop's see.—*Herbert's Life of Henry VIII.*

In the epilogue to this play it is recommended

> To the merciful construction of good women,
> For *such a one* we shewed 'em :

alluding to the character of Queen Katherine. Shakespeare has, in fact, placed before us a queen and a heroine, who in the first place, and above all, is a *good* woman ; and I repeat, that in doing so, and in trusting for all his effect to truth and virtue, he has given a sublime proof of his genius and his wisdom ;—for which, among many other obligations, we women remain his debtors.

[*From Hazlitt's* "*Characters of Shakespeare.*"]

This play contains little action or violence of passion, yet it has considerable interest of a more mild and thoughtful cast, and some of the most striking passages in the author's works. The character of Queen Katherine is the most perfect delineation of matronly dignity, sweetness, and resignation that can be conceived. Her appeals to the protection of the king, her remonstrances to the cardinals, her conversations with her women, show a noble and generous spirit, accompanied with the utmost gentleness of nature. What can be more affecting than her answer to Campeius and Wolsey, who come to visit her as pretended friends ?—

> " Nay, forsooth, my friends,
> They that must weigh out my afflictions,
> They that my trust must grow to, live not here ;
> They are, as all my other comforts, far hence,
> In mine own country, lords."

Dr. Johnson observes of this play that "the meek sorrows and virtuous distress of Katherine have furnished some scenes which may be justly numbered among the greatest efforts of tragedy. But the genius of Shakespeare comes in and goes out with Katherine. Every other part may be easily conceived and easily written." This is easily said ; but, with all due deference to so great a reputed authority as that of Johnson, it is not true. For instance, the scene of Buckingham led to execution is one of the most affecting and natural in Shakespeare, and to which there is hardly an approach in any other author. Again, the character of Wolsey, the description of his pride and fall, are inimitable, and have, besides their gorgeousness of effect, a pathos which only the genius of Shakespeare could lend to the distresses of a proud, bad man, like Wolsey. There is a sort of child-like simplicity in the very helplessness of his situation, arising from the recollection of his past overbearing ambition. After the cutting sarcasms of his enemies on his disgrace, against which he bears up with a spirit conscious of his own superiority, he breaks out into that fine apostrophe, "Farewell, a long farewell to all my greatness!" etc. There is in this passage, as well as in the well-known dialogue with Cromwell which follows, something which stretches beyond commonplace; nor is the account which Griffith gives of Wolsey's death less Shakespearian; and the candour with which Queen Katherine listens to the praise of "him whom I most hated living," adds the last graceful finishing to her character.

[*From Knight's Comments on the Play.**]

"I come no more to make you laugh; things now
That bear a weighty and a serious brow,
Sad, high, and working, full of state and woe,
Such noble scenes as draw the eye to flow,
We now present."

This is the commencement of the most remarkable Prologue of the few which are attached to Shakespeare's plays. It is, to our minds, a perfect exposition of the principle upon which the poet worked in the construction of this drama. Believing, whatever weight of authority there may be for the contrary opinion, that the *Henry VIII.* was a new play in

* *Pictorial Edition of Shakespeare: Histories*, vol. ii., p. 394 foll.

1613, there had been a considerable interval between its production and that of *Henry V.*, the last in the order of representation of his previous Histories. During that interval several of the poet's most admirable comedies had been unquestionably produced; and the audience of 1613 was perhaps still revelling in the recollections of the wit of Touchstone or the more recent whimsies of Autolycus. But the poet, who was equally master of the tears and the smiles of his audience, prepares them for a serious view of the aspects of real life—"I come no more to make you laugh." He thought, too, that the popular desire for noisy combats, and the unavoidable deficiencies of the stage in the representation of battle-scenes—he had before described it as an "unworthy scaffold" for "vasty fields"—might be passingly adverted to; and that the clowns of the same stage, whom he had indeed reformed, but who still delighted the "ears of the groundlings" with their extemporal rudeness, might be slightly renounced. He disclaimed, then, "both fool and fight;" these were not among the attractions of this work of his maturer age. He had to offer weighty and serious things; sad and high things; noble scenes that commanded tears; state and woe were to be exhibited together; there was to be pageantry, but it was to be full of pity; and the woe was to be the more intense from its truth. And how did this master of his art profess to be able to produce such deep emotion from the exhibition of scenes that almost came down to his own times; that the fathers and grandfathers of his audience had witnessed in their unpoetical reality; that belonged, not to the period when the sword was the sole arbiter of the destinies of princes and favourites, but when men fell by intrigue and not by battle, and even the axe of the capricious despot struck in the name of the law? There was another great poet of this age of high poetry who had indicated the general theme which Shakespeare proposed to illustrate in this drama:—

"What man that sees the ever-whirling wheele
Of change, the which all mortall things doth sway,
But that therby doth find, and plainly feele,
How MUTABILITY in them doth play
Her cruell sports to many mens decay?"*

From the first scene to the last, the dramatic action seems to point to the abiding presence of that power which works "her cruel sports to many men's decay." We see "the ever-whirling wheel" in a succession of contrasts of grandeur and debasement; and, even when the action is closed, we are carried forward into the depths of the future, to have the same triumph of "mutability" suggested to our contemplation. This is the theme which the poet emphatically presents to us under its aspect of sadness:

"Be sad as we would make ye. Think ye see
The very persons of our noble story,
As they were living; think you see them great,
And follow'd with the general throng and sweat
Of thousand friends; then in a moment see
How soon this mightiness meets misery."

[*From Hudson's Introduction to the Play.*†]

The main idea of this play, that whereon the grouping of the persons and the casting of the parts are made to proceed, is announced in the Prologue, thus:

"You see them great,
And follow'd with the general throng and sweat
Of thousand friends; then in a moment see
How soon this mightiness meets misery."

Here we have the key-note of the whole, that which draws and tempers the several particulars into consistency and harmony of effect. Accordingly, the interest turns on a series of sudden and most affecting reverses. One after another the mighty are humbled and the lofty laid low, their pros-

* Spenser's *Faerie Queene:* Two Cantos of Mutabilitie.
† Hudson's *Shakespeare*, vol. vii., p. 202.

perity being strained to a high pitch, as if on purpose to deepen their plunge, just when they have reached the summit, with their hearts built up and settled to the height of their rising, and when the wheel of Fortune seems fast locked, with themselves at the top. . . .

Yet, in all these cases, because the persons have their greatness inherent and not adventitious, therefore they carry it with them in their reverses; or, rather, in seeming to lose it, they augment it. For it is then seen, as it could not be before, that the greatness which was in their circumstances only served to cripple or obscure that which was in themselves; their nobler and better qualities shining out afresh when they are brought low, so that from their fall we learn the real causes of their rising. . . .

Nor is the change in our feelings toward them, after their fall, merely an effect passing within ourselves: it proceeds, in part, upon a disclosure and outcoming of somewhat in them that was before hidden or stifled beneath the superinducings of place and circumstances; it is the seeing what they really are, and not merely the considering what they have lost, that now moves us to do them reverence; for those elements which, stimulated into an usurped predominance by the subtly-working drugs of flattery and pride, before made them hateful and repulsive, are now overmastered by the stronger elements of good that have their dwelling in them. And because this is real and true, exaltation springs up as the natural consequence of their overthrow; therefore it is that from the ruins of their fallen state the poet builds "such noble scenes as draw the eye to flow."

WOLSEY'S HALF GROAT.

HALL IN BLACK-FRIARS [Act II., Scene 4].

KING HENRY THE EIGHTH.

DRAMATIS PERSONÆ.

KING HENRY THE EIGHTH.
CARDINAL WOLSEY.
CARDINAL CAMPEIUS.
CAPUCIUS, Ambassador from Charles V.
CRANMER, Archbishop of Canterbury.
DUKE OF NORFOLK.
DUKE OF BUCKINGHAM.
DUKE OF SUFFOLK.
EARL OF SURREY.
Lord Chamberlain.
Lord Chancellor.
GARDINER, Bishop of Winchester.
Bishop of Lincoln.
LORD ABERGAVENNY.
LORD SANDS.
Sir HENRY GUILDFORD.
Sir THOMAS LOVELL.
Sir ANTHONY DENNY.
Sir NICHOLAS VAUX.
Secretaries to Wolsey.
CROMWELL, Servant to Wolsey.
GRIFFITH, Gentleman Usher to Queen Katherine.
Three other Gentlemen. Garter King at Arms.
Doctor BUTTS, Physician to the King.
Surveyor to the Duke of Buckingham.
BRANDON, and a Sergeant at Arms.
Door-keeper of the Council Chamber. Porter and his Man. Page to Gardiner. A Crier.

QUEEN KATHERINE, Wife to King Henry.
ANNE BULLEN, her Maid of Honor, afterward Queen.
An old Lady, Friend to Anne Bullen.
PATIENCE, Woman to Queen Katherine.

Several Lords and Ladies in the Dumb Shows; Women attending upon the Queen; Spirits, which appear to her; Scribes, Officers, Guards, and other Attendants.

SCENE: *Chiefly in London and Westminster; once at Kimbolton.*

THE TOWER FROM THE THAMES.

PROLOGUE.

I COME no more to make you laugh: things now
That bear a weighty and a serious brow,
Sad, high, and working, full of state and woe,
Such noble scenes as draw the eye to flow,
We now present. Those that can pity, here
May, if they think it well, let fall a tear;
The subject will deserve it. Such as give

Their money out of hope they may believe,
May here find truth too. Those that come to see
Only a show or two, and so agree
The play may pass, if they be still and willing,
I'll undertake may see away their shilling
Richly in two short hours. Only they
That come to hear a merry, bawdy play,
A noise of targets, or to see a fellow
In a long motley coat, guarded with yellow,
Will be deceiv'd; for, gentle hearers, know,
To rank our chosen truth with such a show
As fool and fight is, beside forfeiting
Our own brains, and the opinion that we bring
(To make that only true we now intend),
Will leave us never an understanding friend.
Therefore, for goodness' sake, and as you are known
The first and happiest hearers of the town,
Be sad as we would make ye: think ye see
The very persons of our noble story
As they were living; think you see them great,
And follow'd with the general throng and sweat
Of thousand friends; then, in a moment, see
How soon this mightiness meets misery:
And if you can be merry then, I'll say
A man may weep upon his wedding day.

PRESENCE-CHAMBER IN YORK-PLACE.

ACT I.

SCENE I. *London. An Ante-chamber in the Palace.*

Enter the DUKE OF NORFOLK *at one door; at the other, the* DUKE OF BUCKINGHAM *and the* LORD ABERGAVENNY.

Buckingham. Good morrow, and well met. How have you done
Since last we saw in France?

Norfolk. I thank your grace,
Healthful; and ever since a fresh admirer
Of what I saw there.
Buckingham. An untimely ague
Stay'd me a prisoner in my chamber, when
Those suns of glory, those two lights of men,
Met in the vale of Andren.
Norfolk. 'Twixt Guynes and Arde:
I was then present, saw them salute on horseback;
Beheld them when they lighted, how they clung
In their embracement, as they grew together;
Which had they, what four thron'd ones could have weigh'd
Such a compounded one?
Buckingham. All the whole time
I was my chamber's prisoner.
Norfolk. Then you lost
The view of earthly glory: men might say
Till this time, pomp was single, but now married
To one above itself. Each following day
Became the next day's master, till the last
Made former wonders it's: to-day the French,
All clinquant, all in gold, like heathen gods,
Shone down the English; and to-morrow they
Made Britain India: every man that stood
Shew'd like a mine. Their dwarfish pages were
As cherubins, all gilt: the madams, too,
Not us'd to toil, did almost sweat to bear
The pride upon them, that their very labour
Was to them as a painting: now this mask
Was cried incomparable; and th' ensuing night
Made it a fool and beggar. The two kings,
Equal in lustre, were now best, now worst,
As presence did present them; him in eye,
Still him in praise; and, being present both,
'Twas said they saw but one: and no discerner

Durst wag his tongue in censure. When these suns
(For so they phrase 'em) by their heralds challeng'd
The noble spirits to arms, they did perform
Beyond thought's compass; that former fabulous story,
Being now seen possible enough, got credit,
That Bevis was believ'd.

Buckingham. O, you go far.

Norfolk. As I belong to worship, and affect
In honour honesty, the tract of every thing
Would by a good discourser lose some life,
Which action's self was tongue to. All was royal:
To the disposing of it naught rebell'd;
Order gave each thing view; the office did
Distinctly his full function.

Buckingham. Who did guide,
I mean who set the body and the limbs
Of this great sport together, as you guess?

Norfolk. One, certes, that promises no element
In such a business.

Buckingham. I pray you, who, my lord?

Norfolk. All this was order'd by the good discretion
Of the right reverend Cardinal of York.

Buckingham. The devil speed him! no man's pie is freed
From his ambitious finger. What had he
To do in these fierce vanities? I wonder
That such a keech can, with his very bulk,
Take up the rays o' th' beneficial sun,
And keep it from the earth.

Norfolk. Surely, sir,
There's in him stuff that puts him to these ends;
For, being not propp'd by ancestry, whose grace
Chalks successors their way, nor call'd upon
For high feats done to th' crown, neither allied
To eminent assistants, but, spider-like,
Out of his self-drawing web, he gives us note,

The force of his own merit makes his way;
A gift that heaven gives for him, which buys
A place next to the king.

Abergavenny. I cannot tell
What heaven hath given him: let some graver eye
Pierce into that; but I can see his pride
Peep through each part of him: whence has he that?
If not from hell, the devil is a niggard,
Or has given all before, and he begins
A new hell in himself.

Buckingham. Why the devil,
Upon this French going-out, took he upon him
(Without the privity o' th' king) t' appoint
Who should attend on him? He makes up the file
Of all the gentry; for the most part such
To whom as great a charge as little honour
He meant to lay upon: and his own letter
(The honorable board of council out)
Must fetch him in he papers.

Abergavenny. I do know
Kinsmen of mine, three at the least, that have
By this so sicken'd their estates, that never
They shall abound as formerly.

Buckingham. O, many
Have broke their backs with laying manors on 'em
For this great journey. What did this vanity
But minister communication of
A most poor issue?

Norfolk. Grievingly I think,
The peace between the French and us not values
The cost that did conclude it.

Buckingham. Every man,
After the hideous storm that follow'd, was
A thing inspir'd; and, not consulting, broke
Into a general prophecy,—that this tempest,

Dashing the garment of this peace, aboded
The sudden breach on't.
  Norfolk. Which is budded out;
For France hath flaw'd the league, and hath attach'd
Our merchants' goods at Bourdeaux.
  Abergavenny. Is it therefore
Th' ambassador is silenc'd?
  Norfolk. Marry, is't.
  Abergavenny. A proper title of a peace, and purchas'd
At a superfluous rate.
  Buckingham. Why, all this business
Our reverend cardinal carried.
  Norfolk. Like it your grace,
The state takes notice of the private difference
Betwixt you and the cardinal. I advise you
(And take it from a heart that wishes towards you
Honour and plenteous safety) that you read
The cardinal's malice and his potency
Together; to consider further that
What his high hatred would effect wants not
A minister in his power. You know his nature,
That he's revengeful; and, I know, his sword
Hath a sharp edge: it's long, and't may be said,
It reaches far; and where 'twill not extend,
Thither he darts it. Bosom up my counsel;
You'll find it wholesome.—Lo, where comes that rock,
That I advise your shunning.

Enter CARDINAL WOLSEY (*the purse borne before him*), *certain of the* Guard, *and two* Secretaries *with papers. The Cardinal in his passage fixeth his eye on Buckingham, and Buckingham on him, both full of disdain.*

  Wolsey. The Duke of Buckingham's surveyor? ha!
Where's his examination?
  1 *Secretary.* Here, so please you.

Wolsey. Is he in person ready?
1 *Secretary.* Ay, please your grace.
Wolsey. Well, we shall then know more; and Buckingham
Shall lessen this big look. [*Exeunt Wolsey and train.*
Buckingham. This butcher's cur is venom-mouth'd, and I
Have not the power to muzzle him; therefore, best
Not wake him in his slumber. A beggar's book
Out-worths a noble's blood.
Norfolk. What, are you chaf'd?
Ask God for temp'rance; that's th' appliance only
Which your disease requires.
Buckingham. I read in's looks
Matter against me; and his eye revil'd
Me, as his abject object: at this instant
He bores me with some trick. He's gone t' th' king:
I'll follow and out-stare him.
Norfolk. Stay, my lord,
And let your reason with your choler question
What 'tis you go about. To climb steep hills,
Requires slow pace at first: anger is like
A full-hot horse, who being allow'd his way,
Self-mettle tires him. Not a man in England
Can advise me like you: be to yourself
As you would to your friend.
Buckingham. I'll to the king;
And from a mouth of honour quite cry down
This Ipswich fellow's insolence, or proclaim
There's difference in no persons.
Norfolk. Be advis'd;
Heat not a furnace for your foe so hot
That it do singe yourself: we may outrun
By violent swiftness that which we run at,
And lose by over-running. Know you not
The fire that mounts the liquor till't run o'er,
In seeming to augment it wastes it? Be advis'd:

I say again, there is no English soul
More stronger to direct you than yourself,
If with the sap of reason you would quench,
Or but allay, the fire of passion.
Buckingham. Sir,
I am thankful to you, and I'll go along
By your prescription ; but this top-proud fellow,
Whom from the flow of gall I name not, but
From sincere motions, by intelligence
And proofs as clear as founts in July, when
We see each grain of gravel, I do know
To be corrupt and treasonous.
Norfolk. Say not treasonous.
Buckingham. To th' king I'll say't, and make my vouch as strong
As shore of rock. Attend. This holy fox,
Or wolf, or both (for he is equal ravenous
As he is subtle, and as prone to mischief
As able to perform't,—his mind and place
Infecting one another, yea, reciprocally),
Only to shew his pomp, as well in France
As here at home, suggests the king, our master,
To this last costly treaty, th' interview
That swallowed so much treasure, and like a glass
Did break i' th' rinsing.
Norfolk. Faith, and so it did.
Buckingham. Pray give me favour, sir. This cunning cardinal
The articles o' th' combination drew
As himself pleas'd ; and they were ratified,
As he cried, "Thus let be," to as much end
As give a crutch t' th' dead. But our count-cardinal
Has done this, and 'tis well ; for worthy Wolsey,
Who cannot err, he did it. Now this follows
(Which, as I take it, is a kind of puppy
To th' old dam, treason), Charles the emperor,

Under pretence to see the queen, his aunt
(For 'twas, indeed, his colour, but he came
To whisper Wolsey), here makes visitation:
His fears were that the interview betwixt
England and France might, through their amity,
Breed him some prejudice; for from this league
Peep'd harms that menac'd him. He privily
Deals with our cardinal, and, as I trow,—
Which I do well; for, I am sure, the emperor
Paid ere he promis'd, whereby his suit was granted
Ere it was ask'd:—but when the way was made,
And pav'd with gold, the emperor thus desir'd,—
That he would please to alter the king's course,
And break the foresaid peace. Let the king know
(As soon he shall by me) that thus the cardinal
Does buy and sell his honour as he pleases,
And for his own advantage.

Norfolk. I am sorry
To hear this of him; and could wish he were
Something mistaken in't.

Buckingham. No, not a syllable:
I do pronounce him in that very shape
He shall appear in proof.

Enter BRANDON; *a* Sergeant at Arms *before him, and two or three of the* Guard.

Brandon. Your office, sergeant; execute it.

Sergeant. Sir,
My lord the Duke of Buckingham, and Earl
Of Hereford, Stafford, and Northampton, I
Arrest thee of high treason, in the name
Of our most sovereign king.

Buckingham. Lo, you, my lord!
The net has fall'n upon me: I shall perish
Under device and practice.

Brandon. I am sorry
To see you ta'en from liberty to look on
The business present. 'Tis his highness' pleasure
You shall to th' Tower.

Buckingham. It will help me nothing
To plead mine innocence; for that dye is on me
Which makes my whit'st part black. The will of heaven
Be done in this and all things!—I obey.—
O, my Lord Aberga'ny, fare you well!

Brandon. Nay, he must bear you company.—The king
[*To Abergavenny.*
Is pleas'd you shall to the Tower, till you know
How he determines further.

Abergavenny. As the duke said,
The will of heaven be done, and the king's pleasure
By me obey'd!

Brandon. Here is a warrant from
The king t' attach Lord Montacute; and the bodies
Of the duke's confessor, John de la Car,
One Gilbert Peck, his chancellor,—

Buckingham. So, so;
These are the limbs o' th' plot. No more, I hope.

Brandon. A monk o' th' Chartreux.

Buckingham. O, Nicholas Hopkins?

Brandon. He.

Buckingham. My surveyor is false: the o'er-great cardinal
Hath shew'd him gold. My life is spann'd already:
I am the shadow of poor Buckingham,
Whose figure even this instant cloud puts on,
By dark'ning my clear sun.—My lord, farewell. [*Exeunt.*

SCENE. II. *The Council-chamber.*

Cornets. Enter KING HENRY, CARDINAL WOLSEY, *the* Lords of the Council, SIR THOMAS LOVELL, Officers, Attendant. *The King enters leaning on the Cardinal's shoulder.*

King Henry. My life itself, and the best heart of it,
Thanks you for this great care. I stood i' th' level
Of a full charg'd confederacy, and give thanks
To you that chok'd it.—Let be call'd before us
That gentleman of Buckingham's: in person
I'll hear him his confessions justify;
And point by point the treasons of his master
He shall again relate.

[*The King takes his seat. The Lords of the Council occupy their several places. The Cardinal places himself under the King's feet, on his right side.*

A noise within, crying, "Room for the Queen." *Enter the* Queen, *ushered by the* DUKES *of* NORFOLK *and* SUFFOLK: *she kneels. The King riseth from his state, takes her up, kisses, and placeth her by him.*

Queen Katherine. Nay, we must longer kneel: I am a suitor.

King Henry. Arise, and take place by us.—Half your suit
Never name to us; you have half our power:
The other moiety, ere you ask, is given;
Repeat your will, and take it.

Queen Katherine. Thank your majesty.
That you would love yourself, and in that love
Not unconsider'd leave your honour, nor
The dignity of your office, is the point
Of my petition.

King Henry. Lady mine, proceed.

Queen Katherine. I am solicited not by a few,
And those of true condition, that your subjects

Are in great grievance. There have been commissions
Sent down among 'em, which hath flaw'd the heart
Of all their loyalties: wherein, although,
My good lord cardinal, they vent reproaches
Most bitterly on you, as putter-on
Of these exactions, yet the king our master,
(Whose honour heaven shield from soil!) even he escapes
not
Language unmannerly; yea, such which breaks
The sides of loyalty, and almost appears
In loud rebellion.

Norfolk. Not almost appears,—
It doth appear; for upon these taxations,
The clothiers all, not able to maintain
The many to them longing, have put off
The spinsters, carders, fullers, weavers, who,
Unfit for other life, compell'd by hunger
And lack of other means, in desperate manner
Daring th' event to th' teeth, are all in uproar,
And danger serves among them.

King Henry. Taxation!
Wherein? and what taxation?—My lord cardinal,
You that are blam'd for it alike with us,
Know you of this taxation?

Wolsey. Please you, sir,
I know but of a single part, in aught
Pertains to th' state; and front but in that file
Where others tell steps with me.

Queen Katherine. No, my lord,
You know no more than others; but you frame
Things, that are known alike, which are not wholesome
To those which would not know them, and yet must
Perforce be their acquaintance. These exactions,
Whereof my sovereign would have note, they are
Most pestilent to th' hearing; and, to bear 'em,

The back is sacrifice to th' load. They say
They are devis'd by you, or else you suffer
Too hard an exclamation.

King Henry. Still exaction!
The nature of it? In what kind, let's know,
Is this exaction?

Queen Katherine. I am much too venturous
In tempting of your patience; but am bolden'd
Under your promis'd pardon. The subjects' grief
Comes through commissions, which compel from each
The sixth part of his substance, to be levied
Without delay; and the pretence for this
Is nam'd—your wars in France. This makes bold mouths:
Tongues spit their duties out, and cold hearts freeze
Allegiance in them: their curses now
Live where their prayers did; and it's come to pass,
This tractable obedience is a slave
To each incensed will. I would your highness
Would give it quick consideration, for
There is no primer business.

King Henry. By my life,
This is against our pleasure.

Wolsey. And for me,
I have no further gone in this than by
A single voice, and that not pass'd me but
By learned approbation of the judges. If I am
Traduc'd by ignorant tongues, which neither know
My faculties, nor person, yet will be
The chronicles of my doing, let me say,
'Tis but the fate of place, and the rough brake
That virtue must go through. We must not stint
Our necessary actions, in the fear
To cope malicious censurers; which ever,
As ravenous fishes, do a vessel follow
That is new trimm'd, but benefit no further

Than vainly longing. What we oft do best,
By sick interpreters (once weak ones) is
Not ours, or not allow'd ; what worst, as oft,
Hitting a grosser quality, is cried up
For our best act. If we shall stand still,
In fear our motion will be mock'd or carp'd at,
We should take root here, where we sit, or sit
State statues only.
King Henry. Things done well,
And with a care, exempt themselves from fear:
Things done without example, in their issue
Are to be fear'd. Have you a precedent
Of this commission? I believe not any.
We must not rend our subjects from our laws,
And stick them in our will. Sixth part of each?
A trembling contribution! Why, we take
From every tree lop, bark, and part o' th' timber;
And, though we leave it with a root thus hack'd,
The air will drink the sap. To every county
Where this is question'd, send our letters with
Free pardon to each man that has denied
The force of this commission. Pray look to't;
I put it to your care.
Wolsey. A word with you. [*To the Secretary.*
Let there be letters writ to every shire,
Of the king's grace and pardon. The griev'd commons
Hardly conceive of me: let it be nois'd
That through our intercession this revokement
And pardon comes. I shall anon advise you
Further in the proceeding. [*Exit Secretary.*

Enter Surveyor.

Queen Katherine. I am sorry that the Duke of Buckingham
Is run in your displeasure.
King Henry. It grieves many:

The gentleman is learn'd, and a most rare speaker;
To nature none more bound; his training such
That he may furnish and instruct great teachers,
And never seek for aid out of himself: yet see,
When these so noble benefits shall prove
Not well dispos'd, the mind growing once corrupt,
They turn to vicious forms, ten times more ugly
Than ever they were fair. This man so complete,
Who was enroll'd 'mongst wonders, and when we,
Almost with ravish'd listening, could not find
His hour of speech a minute; he, my lady,
Hath into monstrous habits put the graces
That once were his, and is become as black
As if besmear'd in hell. Sit by us; you shall hear
(This was his gentleman in trust) of him
Things to strike honour sad.—Bid him recount
The fore-recited practices, whereof
We cannot feel too little, hear too much.

Wolsey. Stand forth; and with bold spirit relate what you,
Most like a careful subject, have collected
Out of the Duke of Buckingham.

King Henry. Speak freely.

Surveyor. First, it was usual with him, every day
It would infect his speech,—that if the king
Should without issue die, he'll carry it so
To make the sceptre his. These very words
I've heard him utter to his son-in-law,
Lord Aberga'ny, to whom by oath he menac'd
Revenge upon the cardinal.

Wolsey. Please your highness, note
This dangerous conception in this point.
Not friended by his wish, to your high person
His will is most malignant; and it stretches
Beyond you, to your friends.

Queen Katherine. My learn'd lord cardinal,
Deliver all with charity.
King Henry. Speak on.
How grounded he his title to the crown,
Upon our fail? to this point hast thou heard him
At any time speak aught?
Surveyor. He was brought to this
By a vain prophecy of Nicholas Henton.
King Henry. What was that Henton?
Surveyor. Sir, a Chartreux friar,
His confessor; who fed him every minute
With words of sovereignty.
King Henry. How know'st thou this?
Surveyor. Not long before your highness sped to France,
The duke, being at the Rose, within the parish
Saint Lawrence Poultney, did of me demand
What was the speech among the Londoners
Concerning the French journey? I replied,
Men fear'd the French would prove perfidious,
To the king's danger. Presently the duke
Said 'twas the fear, indeed; and that he doubted
'Twould prove the verity of certain words
Spoke by a holy monk; "that oft," says he,
"Hath sent to me, wishing me to permit
John de la Car, my chaplain, a choice hour
To hear from him a matter of some moment:
Whom after, under the confession's seal,
He solemnly had sworn that what he spoke
My chaplain to no creature living but
To me should utter, with demure confidence
This pausingly ensued,—Neither the king nor 's heirs
(Tell you the duke) shall prosper: bid him strive
To gain the love o' th' commonalty: the duke
Shall govern England."
Queen Katherine. If I know you well,

You were the duke's surveyor, and lost your office
On the complaint o' th' tenants : take good heed
You charge not in your spleen a noble person,
And spoil your nobler soul. I say, take heed ;
Yes, heartily beseech you.

King Henry. Let him on.—
Go forward.

Surveyor. On my soul, I'll speak but truth.
I told my lord the duke, by the devil's illusions
The monk might be deceiv'd ; and that 'twas dangerous for him
To ruminate on this so far, until
It forg'd him some design, which, being believ'd,
It was much like to do. He answer'd, "Tush !
It can do me no damage :" adding further,
That had the king in his last sickness fail'd,
The cardinal's and Sir Thomas Lovell's heads
Should have gone off.

King Henry. Ha ! what, so rank ? Ah, ha !
There's mischief in this man.—Canst thou say further ?

Surveyor. I can, my liege.

King Henry. Proceed.

Surveyor. Being at Greenwich,
After your highness had reprov'd the duke
About Sir William Blomer,—

King Henry. I remember
Of such a time : being my sworn servant
The duke retain'd him his.—But on : what hence ?

Surveyor. "If," quoth he, "I for this had been committed,—
As to the Tower I thought,—I would have play'd
The part my father meant to act upon
Th' usurper Richard ; who, being at Salisbury,
Made suit to come in 's presence ; which if granted,
As he made semblance of his duty, would
Have put his knife into him."

King Henry. A giant traitor!

Wolsey. Now, madam, may his highness live in freedom,
And this man out of prison?

Queen Katherine. God mend all!

King Henry. There's something more would out of thee: what say'st?

Surveyor. After "the duke his father," with "the knife,"
He stretch'd him, and, with one hand on his dagger,
Another spread on 's breast, mounting his eyes,
He did discharge a horrible oath; whose tenor
Was,—were he evil us'd, he would out-go
His father by as much as a performance
Does an irresolute purpose.

King Henry. There's his period,
To sheathe his knife in us. He is attach'd;
Call him to present trial: if he may
Find mercy in the law, 'tis his; if none,
Let him not seek 't of us. By day and night,
He's traitor to the height. [*Exeunt.*

SCENE III. *A Room in the Palace.*

Enter the Lord Chamberlain *and* LORD SANDS.

Chamberlain. Is't possible the spells of France should juggle
Men into such strange mysteries?

Sands. New customs,
Though they be never so ridiculous,
Nay, let 'em be unmanly, yet are follow'd.

Chamberlain. As far as I see, all the good our English
Have got by the late voyage is but merely
A fit or two o' th' face; but they are shrewd ones;
For when they hold 'em, you would swear directly
Their very noses had been counsellors
To Pepin or Clotharius, they keep state so.

Sands. They have all new legs, and lame ones: one would take it,
That never saw 'em pace before, the spavin
Or springhalt reign'd among 'em.
Chamberlain. Death! my lord,
Their clothes are after such a pagan cut too,
That, sure, they've worn out Christendom. How now?
What news, Sir Thomas Lovell?

Enter SIR THOMAS LOVELL.

Lovell. Faith, my lord,
I hear of none but the new proclamation
That's clapp'd upon the court-gate.
Chamberlain. What is't for?
Lovell. The reformation of our travell'd gallants
That fill the court with quarrels, talk, and tailors.
Chamberlain. I'm glad 'tis there: now, I would pray our *monsieurs*
To think an English courtier may be wise,
And never see the Louvre.
Lovell. They must either
(For so run the conditions) leave those remnants
Of fool and feather that they got in France,
With all their honourable points of ignorance
Pertaining thereunto, as fights and fireworks;
Abusing better men than they can be,
Out of a foreign wisdom; renouncing clean
The faith they have in tennis, and tall stockings,
Short blister'd breeches, and those types of travel,
And understand again like honest men,
Or pack to their old playfellows: there, I take it,
They may, *cum privilegio*, wear away
The lag end of their lewdness, and be laugh'd at.
Sands. 'Tis time to give 'em physic, their diseases
Are grown so catching.

Chamberlain. What a loss our ladies
Will have of these trim vanities!
Lovell. Ay, marry,
There will be woe, indeed.
Sands. I am glad they're going,
For, sure, there's no converting of 'em: now,
An honest country lord, as I am, beaten
A long time out of play, may bring his plain-song,
And have an hour of hearing, and, by'r Lady,
Held current music too.
Chamberlain. Well said, Lord Sands:
Your colt's tooth is not cast yet.
Sands. No, my lord;
Nor shall not, while I have a stump.
Chamberlain. Sir Thomas,
Whither were you a going?
Lovell. To the cardinal's.
Your lordship is a guest too.
Chamberlain. O, 'tis true:
This night he makes a supper, and a great one,
To many lords and ladies; there will be
The beauty of this kingdom, I'll assure you.
Lovell. That churchman bears a bounteous mind indeed,
A hand as fruitful as the land that feeds us:
His dews fall every where.
Chamberlain. No doubt, he's noble;
He had a black mouth that said other of him.
Sands. He may, my lord; has wherewithal: in him
Sparing would show a worse sin than ill doctrine.
Men of his way should be most liberal;
They are set here for examples.
Chamberlain. True, they are so;
But few now give so great ones. My barge stays;
Your lordship shall along:—Come, good Sir Thomas,
We shall be late else; which I would not be,

For I was spoke to, with Sir Henry Guildford,
This night to be comptrollers.
Sands. I am your lordship's.
[*Exeunt.*

SCENE IV. *The Presence-chamber in York-place.*

Hautboys. A small table under a state for the Cardinal, a longer table for the guests; then enter ANNE BULLEN, *and divers* Lords, Ladies, *and* Gentlewomen, *as guests, at one door; at another door enter* SIR HENRY GUILDFORD.

Guildford. Ladies, a general welcome from his grace
Salutes ye all: this night he dedicates
To fair contènt and you. None here, he hopes,
In all this noble bevy, has brought with her
One care abroad: he would have all as merry
As first good company, good wine, good welcome
Can make good people.—O my lord! you're tardy;

Enter Lord Chamberlain, LORD SANDS, *and* SIR THOMAS LOVELL.

The very thought of this fair company
Clapp'd wings to me.
Chamberlain. You are young, Sir Harry Guildford.—
Sweet ladies, will it please you sit? Sir Harry,
Place you that side, I'll take the charge of this:
His grace is entering.—Nay, you must not freeze;
Two women plac'd together makes cold weather:—
My Lord Sands, you are one will keep 'em waking;
Pray, sit between these ladies.
Sands. By my faith,
And thank your lordship.—By your leave, sweet ladies:
[*Seats himself between Anne Bullen and another lady.*
If I chance to talk a little wild, forgive me;
I had it from my father.

Anne. Was he mad, sir?
Sands. O, very mad, exceeding mad; in love too;
But he would bite none: just as I do now,
He would kiss you twenty with a breath. [*Kisses her.*
Chamberlain. Well said, my lord.—
So now you are fairly seated.—Gentlemen,
The penance lies on you, if these fair ladies
Pass away frowning.
Sands. For my little cure,
Let me alone.

Hautboys. Enter CARDINAL WOLSEY, *attended, and takes his state.*

Wolsey. Ye're welcome, my fair guests: that noble lady,
Or gentleman, that is not freely merry,
Is not my friend. This to confirm my welcome;
And to you all good health. [*Drinks.*
Sands. Your grace is noble:
Let me have such a bowl may hold my thanks,
And save me so much talking.
Wolsey. My Lord Sands,
I am beholding to you: cheer your neighbours.—
Ladies, you are not merry:—gentlemen,
Whose fault is this?
Sands. The red wine first must rise
In their fair cheeks, my lord; then we shall have 'em
Talk us to silence.
Anne. You are a merry gamester,
My Lord Sands.
Sands. Yes, if I make my play.
Here's to your ladyship; and pledge it, madam,
For 'tis to such a thing,—
Anne. You cannot shew me.
Sands. I told your grace they would talk anon.
[*Drum and trumpets within: chambers discharged.*

Wolsey. What's that?

Chamberlain. Look out there, some of ye. [*Exit a Servant.*

Wolsey. What warlike voice,
And to what end is this?—Nay, ladies, fear not;
By all the laws of war ye're privileg'd.

Servant *returns.*

Chamberlain. How now! what is't?

Servant. A noble troop of strangers,
For so they seem: they've left their barge, and landed;
And hither make, as great ambassadors
From foreign princes.

Wolsey. Good lord chamberlain,
Go, give 'em welcome; you can speak the French tongue:
And, pray, receive 'em nobly, and conduct 'em
Into our presence, where this heaven of beauty
Shall shine at full upon them.—Some attend him.—

[*Exit Chamberlain, attended. All arise, and the tables are removed.*

You have now a broken banquet; but we'll mend it.
A good digestion to you all; and, once more,
I shower a welcome on ye.—Welcome all.

Hautboys. Enter the King *and others, as maskers, habited like Shepherds, ushered by the* Lord Chamberlain. *They pass directly before the Cardinal, and gracefully salute him.*

A noble company! what are their pleasures?

Chamberlain. Because they speak no English, thus they pray'd
To tell your grace:—That, having heard by fame
Of this so noble and so fair assembly
This night to meet here, they could do no less,
Out of the great respect they bear to beauty,
But leave their flocks, and under your fair conduct,
Crave leave to view these ladies, and entreat
An hour of revels with 'em.

Wolsey. Say, lord chamberlain,
They have done my poor house grace; for which I pay 'em
A thousand thanks, and pray 'em take their pleasures.
[*Ladies chosen for the dance. The King takes Anne Bullen.*
King Henry. The fairest hand I ever touch'd. O beauty!
Till now I never knew thee. [*Music. Dance.*
Wolsey. My lord,—
Chamberlain. Your grace?
Wolsey. Pray tell 'em thus much from me.
There should be one amongst 'em, by his person,
More worthy this place than myself; to whom,
If I but knew him, with my love and duty
I would surrender it.
Chamberlain. I will, my lord.
[*Chamberlain goes to the maskers, and returns.*
Wolsey. What say they?
Chamberlain. Such a one, they all confess,
There is, indeed; which they would have your grace
Find out, and he will take it.
Wolsey. Let me see then.—
[*Comes from his state.*
By all your good leaves, gentlemen; here I'll make
My royal choice.
King Henry. You have found him, cardinal. [*Unmasks.*
You hold a fair assembly; you do well, lord:
You are a churchman, or, I'll tell you, cardinal,
I should judge now unhappily.
Wolsey. I am glad
Your grace is grown so pleasant.
King Henry. My lord chamberlain,
Prithee, come hither. What fair lady's that?
Chamberlain. An't please your grace, Sir Thomas Bullen's daughter,—
The Viscount Rochford,—one of her highness' women.
King Henry. By heaven she is a dainty one.—Sweetheart,

I were unmannerly to take you out,
And not to kiss you.—A health, gentlemen!
Let it go round.

Wolsey. Sir Thomas Lovell, is the banquet ready
I' th' privy chamber?

Lovell. Yes, my lord.

Wolsey. Your grace,
I fear, with dancing is a little heated.

King Henry. I fear, too much.

Wolsey. There's fresher air, my lord,
In the next chamber.

King Henry. Lead in your ladies, every one.—Sweet part- [ner,
I must not yet forsake you.—Let's be merry,
Good my lord cardinal: I have half a dozen healths
To drink to these fair ladies, and a measure
To lead 'em once again; and then let's dream
Who's best in favour.—Let the music knock it.

[*Exeunt with trumpets.*

MEDAL OF FRANCIS I.

ACT II.

SCENE I. *A Street.*

Enter two Gentlemen, *meeting.*

1 *Gentleman.* Whither away so fast?

2 *Gentleman.* O!—God save ye!

Even to the hall, to hear what shall become
Of the great Duke of Buckingham.
1 *Gentleman.* I'll save you
That labour, sir. All's now done, but the ceremony
Of bringing back the prisoner.
2 *Gentleman.* Were you there?
1 *Gentleman.* Yes, indeed, was I.
2 *Gentleman.* Pray, speak what has happen'd.
1 *Gentleman.* You may guess quickly what.
2 *Gentleman.* Is he found guilty?
1 *Gentleman.* Yes, truly is he, and condemn'd upon't.
2 *Gentleman.* I am sorry for't.
1 *Gentleman.* So are a number more.
2 *Gentleman.* But, pray, how pass'd it?
1 *Gentleman.* I'll tell you in a little. The great duke
Came to the bar; where to his accusations
He pleaded still, not guilty, and alleg'd
Many sharp reasons to defeat the law.
The king's attorney, on the contrary,
Urg'd on the examinations, proofs, confessions
Of divers witnesses, which the duke desir'd
To have brought, *viva voce*, to his face:
At which appear'd against him his surveyor;
Sir Gilbert Peck, his chancellor; and John Car,
Confessor to him; with that devil-monk,
Hopkins, that made this mischief.
2 *Gentleman.* That was he,
That fed him with his prophecies?
1 *Gentleman.* The same.
All these accus'd him strongly; which he fain
Would have flung from him, but, indeed, he could not:
And so his peers, upon this evidence,
Have found him guilty of high treason. Much
He spoke, and learnedly, for life; but all
Was either pitied in him or forgotten.

2 *Gentleman.* After all this, how did he bear himself?
1 *Gentleman.* When he was brought again to th' bar, to hear
His knell rung out, his judgment, he was stirr'd
With such an agony, he sweat extremely,
And something spoke in choler, ill and hasty;
But he fell to himself again, and sweetly
In all the rest shew'd a most noble patience.
2 *Gentleman.* I do not think he fears death.
1 *Gentleman.* Sure, he does not;
He was never so womanish: the cause
He may a little grieve at.
2 *Gentleman.* Certainly,
The cardinal is the end of this.
1 *Gentleman.* 'Tis likely,
By all conjectures: first, Kildare's attainder,
Then deputy of Ireland; who remov'd,
Earl Surrey was sent thither, and in haste too,
Lest he should help his father.
2 *Gentleman.* That trick of state
Was a deep envious one.
1 *Gentleman.* At his return,
No doubt he will requite it. This is noted,
And generally; whoever the king favours,
The cardinal instantly will find employment,
And far enough from court too.
2 *Gentleman.* All the commons
Hate him perniciously, and, o' my conscience,
Wish him ten fathom deep: this duke as much
They love and dote on; call him bounteous Buckingham,
The mirror of all courtesy,—
1 *Gentleman.* Stay there, sir;
And see the noble ruin'd man you speak of.

Enter BUCKINGHAM *from his arraignment; Tipstaves before him: the axe, with the edge towards him: Halberds on each side; accompanied with* Sir Thomas Lovell, Sir Nicholas Vaux, Sir William Sands, *and Common People.*

2 *Gentleman.* Let's stand close, and behold him.

Buckingham. All good people,
You that thus far have come to pity me,
Hear what I say, and then go home and lose me.
I have this day receiv'd a traitor's judgment,
And by that name must die: yet, heaven bear witness,
And if I have a conscience, let it sink me,
Even as the axe falls, if I be not faithful.
The law I bear no malice for my death,
'T has done upon the premises but justice;
But those that sought it I could wish more Christians:
Be what they will, I heartily forgive 'em.
Yet let 'em look they glory not in mischief,
Nor build their evils on the graves of great men;
For then my guiltless blood must cry against 'em.
For further life in this world I ne'er hope,
Nor will I sue, although the king have mercies
More than I dare make faults. You few that lov'd me,
And dare be bold to weep for Buckingham,
His noble friends and fellows, whom to leave
Is only bitter to him only dying,
Go with me, like good angels, to my end;
And, as the long divorce of steel falls on me,
Make of your prayers one sweet sacrifice,
And lift my soul to heaven.—Lead on, o' God's name.

Lovell. I do beseech your grace for charity,
If ever any malice in your heart
Were hid against me, now to forgive me frankly.

Buckingham. Sir Thomas Lovell, I as free forgive you,
As I would be forgiven: I forgive all:
There cannot be those numberless offences
'Gainst me, that I cannot take peace with: no black envy
Shall mark my grave. Commend me to his grace;

And, if he speak of Buckingham, pray tell him,
You met him half in heaven. My vows and prayers
Yet are the king's; and, till my soul forsake,
Shall cry for blessings on him: may he live
Longer than I have time to tell his years!
Ever belov'd and loving may his rule be!
And when old Time shall lead him to his end,
Goodness and he fill up one monument!

Lovell. To the water side I must conduct your grace;
Then give my charge up to Sir Nicholas Vaux,
Who undertakes you to your end.

Vaux. Prepare there!
The duke is coming: see the barge be ready;
And fit it with such furniture as suits
The greatness of his person.

Buckingham. Nay, Sir Nicholas,
Let it alone: my state now will but mock me.
When I came hither, I was Lord High Constable,
And Duke of Buckingham; now, poor Edward Bohun:
Yet I am richer than my base accusers,
That never knew what truth meant. I now seal it;
And with that blood will make 'em one day groan for't.
My noble father, Henry of Buckingham,
Who first rais'd head against usurping Richard,
Flying for succour to his servant Banister,
Being distress'd, was by that wretch betray'd,
And without trial fell. God's peace be with him!
Henry the Seventh succeeding, truly pitying
My father's loss, like a most royal prince,
Restor'd me to my honours, and out of ruins
Made my name once more noble. Now, his son,
Henry the Eighth, life, honour, name, and all
That made me happy, at one stroke has taken
Forever from the world. I had my trial,
And must needs say, a noble one; which makes me

A little happier than my wretched father:
Yet thus far we are one in fortunes,—both
Fell by our servants, by those men we lov'd most:
A most unnatural and faithless service!
Heaven has an end in all: yet, you that hear me,
This from a dying man receive as certain:
Where you are liberal of your loves and counsels,
Be sure you be not loose; for those you make friends,
And give your hearts to, when they once perceive
The least rub in your fortunes, fall away
Like water from ye, never found again
But where they mean to sink ye. All good people,
Pray for me! I must now forsake ye: the last hour
Of my long weary life is come upon me.
Farewell: and when you would say something that is sad,
Speak how I fell.—I have done, and God forgive me.
[*Exeunt Buckingham, etc.*

1 *Gentleman.* O, this is full of pity!—Sir, it calls,
I fear, too many curses on their heads
That were the authors.

2 *Gentleman.* If the duke be guiltless,
'Tis full of woe: yet I can give you inkling
Of an ensuing evil, if it fall,
Greater than this.

1 *Gentleman.* Good angels keep it from us!
What may it be? You do not doubt my faith, sir?

2 *Gentleman.* This secret is so weighty, 'twill require
A strong faith to conceal it.

1 *Gentleman.* Let me have it:
I do not talk much.

2 *Gentleman.* I am confident:
You shall, sir. Did you not of late days hear
A buzzing of a separation
Between the king and Katherine?

1 *Gentleman.* Yes, but it held not;

For when the king once heard it, out of anger
He sent command to the lord mayor straight
To stop the rumour, and allay those tongues
That durst disperse it.
  2 *Gentleman.* But that slander, sir,
Is found a truth now; for it grows again
Fresher than e'er it was, and held for certain
The king will venture at it. Either the cardinal,
Or some about him near, have out of malice
To the good queen, possess'd him with a scruple
That will undo her: to confirm this, too,
Cardinal Campeius is arriv'd, and lately;
As all think, for this business.
  1 *Gentleman.* 'Tis the cardinal;
And merely to revenge him on the emperor,
For not bestowing on him, at his asking,
The archbishopric of Toledo, this is purpos'd. [cruel,
  2 *Gentleman.* I think you have hit the mark: but is't not
That she should feel the smart of this? The cardinal
Will have his will, and she must fall.
  1 *Gentleman.* 'Tis woeful.
We are too open here to argue this;
Let's think in private more. [*Exeunt.*

SCENE II. *An Ante-chamber in the Palace.*

Enter the Lord Chamberlain, *reading a letter.*

Chamberlain. "*My Lord,—The horses your lordship sent for, with all the care I had, I saw well chosen, ridden, and furnish'd. They were young and handsome, and of the best breed in the North. When they were ready to set out for London, a man of my lord cardinal's, by commission and main power, took 'em from me; with this reason,—his master would be serv'd before a subject, if not before the king; which stopp'd our mouths, sir.*"

I fear he will indeed. Well, let him have them:
He will have all, I think.

Enter the DUKES OF NORFOLK *and* SUFFOLK.

Norfolk. Well met, my lord chamberlain.
Chamberlain. Good day to both your graces.
Suffolk. How is the king employ'd?
Chamberlain. I left him private,
Full of sad thoughts and troubles.
Norfolk. What's the cause?
Chamberlain. It seems the marriage with his brother's wife
Has crept too near his conscience.
Suffolk. No; his conscience
Has crept too near another lady.
Norfolk. 'Tis so.
This is the cardinal's doing, the king-cardinal:
That blind priest, like the eldest son of fortune,
Turns what he list. The king will know him one day.
Suffolk. Pray God he do! he'll never know himself else.
Norfolk. How holily he works in all his business,
And with what zeal! for, now he has crack'd the league
Between us and the emperor, the queen's great nephew,
He dives into the king's soul, and there scatters
Dangers, doubts, wringing of the conscience,
Fears and despairs,—and all these for his marriage:
And out of all these to restore the king,
He counsels a divorce: a loss of her,
That like a jewel has hung twenty years
About his neck, yet never lost her lustre;
Of her that loves him with that excellence
That angels love good men with; even of her
That, when the greatest stroke of fortune falls,
Will bless the king. And is not this course pious?
Chamberlain. Heaven keep me from such counsel! 'Tis most true,

These news are every where ; every tongue speaks 'em,
And every true heart weeps for't. All that dare
Look into these affairs see this main end,—
The French king's sister. Heaven will one day open
The king's eyes, that so long have slept upon
This bold bad man.

Suffolk. And free us from his slavery.

Norfolk. We had need pray,
And heartily, for our deliverance,
Or this imperious man will work us all
From princes into pages. All men's honours
Lie like one lump before him, to be fashion'd
Into what pitch he please.

Suffolk. For me, my lords,
I love him not, nor fear him ; there's my creed.
As I am made without him, so I'll stand,
If the king please : his curses and his blessings
Touch me alike ; they're breath I not believe in.
I knew him and I know him ; so I leave him
To him that made him proud, the Pope.

Norfolk. Let's in,
And with some other business put the king
From these sad thoughts, that work too much upon him.—
My lord, you'll bear us company?

Chamberlain. Excuse me ;
The king hath sent me other where : besides,
You'll find a most unfit time to disturb him.
Health to your lordships.

Norfolk. Thanks, my good lord chamberlain.
[*Exit Lord Chamberlain.*

Norfolk opens a folding-door. The King is discovered sitting, and reading pensively.

Suffolk. How sad he looks! sure, he is much afflicted.

King Henry. Who is there, ha?

Norfolk. Pray God he be not angry!
King Henry. Who's there, I say? How dare you thrust yourselves
Into my private meditations?
Who am I? ha!
Norfolk. A gracious king, that pardons all offences
Malice ne'er meant: our breach of duty this way
Is business of estate; in which we come
To know your royal pleasure.
King Henry. Ye are too bold.
Go to; I'll make ye know your times of business:
Is this an hour for temporal affairs, ha?—

Enter WOLSEY *and* CAMPEIUS.

Who's there? my good lord cardinal?—O, my Wolsey,
The quiet of my wounded conscience;
Thou art a cure fit for a king.—You're welcome,
[*To Campeius.*
Most learned reverend sir, into our kingdom:
Use us and it.—[*To Wolsey.*] My good lord, have great care
I be not found a talker.
Wolsey. Sir, you cannot.
I would your grace would give us but an hour
Of private conference.
King Henry. [*To Norfolk and Suffolk.*] We are busy: go.
Norfolk [*Aside, as they retire*]. This priest has no pride in him.
Suffolk. Not to speak of;
I would not be so sick though for his place:
But this cannot continue.
Norfolk. If it do,
I'll venture one have-at-him.
Suffolk. I another.
[*Exeunt Norfolk and Suffolk.*
Wolsey. Your grace has given a precedent of wisdom

Above all princes, in committing freely
Your scruple to the voice of Christendom.
Who can be angry now? what envy reach you?
The Spaniard, tied by blood and favour to her,
Must now confess, if they have any goodness,
The trial just and noble. All the clerks,
I mean the learned ones, in Christian kingdoms
Gave their free voices. Rome, the nurse of judgment,
Invited by your noble self, hath sent
One general tongue unto us, this good man,
This just and learned priest, Cardinal Campeius;
Whom once more I present unto your highness.

King Henry. And once more in mine arms I bid him welcome,
And thank the holy conclave for their loves:
They have sent me such a man I would have wish'd for.

Campeius. Your grace must needs deserve all strangers' loves,
You are so noble. To your highness' hand
I tender my commission; by whose virtue
(The court of Rome commanding) you, my Lord
Cardinal of York, are join'd with me, their servant,
In the unpartial judging of this business.

King Henry. Two equal men. The queen shall be acquainted
Forthwith for what you come.—Where's Gardiner?

Wolsey. I know your majesty has always lov'd her
So dear in heart, not to deny her that
A woman of less place might ask by law,—
Scholars, allow'd freely to argue for her.

King Henry. Ay, and the best she shall have; and my favour
To him that does best: God forbid else! Cardinal,
Prithee, call Gardiner to me, my new secretary:
I find him a fit fellow. [*Exit Wolsey.*

Enter WOLSEY, *with* GARDINER.

Wolsey. Give me your hand; much joy and favour to you:
You are the king's now.
Gardiner. But to be commanded
Forever by your grace, whose hand has rais'd me.
King Henry. Come hither, Gardiner.
[*They walk and whisper.*
Campeius. My Lord of York, was not one Doctor Pace
In this man's place before him?
Wolsey. Yes, he was.
Campeius. Was he not held a learned man?
Wolsey. Yes, surely.
Campeius. Believe me, there's an ill opinion spread, then,
Even of yourself, lord cardinal.
Wolsey. How of me?
Campeius. They will not stick to say you envied him;
And fearing he would rise, he was so virtuous,
Kept him a foreign man still; which so griev'd him
That he ran mad and died.
Wolsey. Heaven's peace be with him!
That's Christian care enough: for living murmurers
There's places of rebuke. He was a fool,
For he would needs be virtuous: that good fellow,
If I command him, follows my appointment;
I will have none so near else. Learn this, brother,
We live not to be grip'd by meaner persons.
King Henry. Deliver this with modesty to the queen.
[*Exit Gardiner.*
The most convenient place that I can think of,
For such receipt of learning, is Black-friars:
There ye shall meet about this weighty business.—
My Wolsey, see it furnish'd.—O my lord!
Would it not grieve an able man to leave

So sweet a bedfellow? But conscience, conscience,—
O, 'tis a tender place! and I must leave her. [*Exeunt.*

SCENE III. *An Ante-chamber in the Queen's Apartments.*

Enter ANNE BULLEN *and an* Old Lady.

Anne. Not for that neither:—here's the pang that pinches;
His highness having liv'd so long with her, and she
So good a lady, that no tongue could ever
Pronounce dishonour of her,—by my life,
She never knew harm-doing;—O, now, after
So many courses of the sun enthron'd,
Still growing in a majesty and pomp, the which
To leave, a thousand-fold more bitter than
'Tis sweet at first t' acquire,—after this process,
To give her the avaunt! it is a pity
Would move a monster.

Old Lady. Hearts of most hard temper
Melt and lament for her.

Anne. O, God's will! much better
She ne'er had known pomp: though 't be temporal,
Yet if that quarrel, Fortune, do divorce
It from the bearer, 'tis a sufferance panging
As soul and body's severing.

Old Lady. Alas, poor lady!
She's a stranger now again.

Anne. So much the more
Must pity drop upon her. Verily,
I swear 'tis better to be lowly born,
And range with humble livers in content,
Than to be perk'd up in a glistering grief,
And wear a golden sorrow.

Old Lady. Our content
Is our best having.

Anne. By my troth and maidenhead,
I would not be a queen.

Old Lady. Beshrew me, I would,
And venture maidenhead for't; and so would you,
For all this spice of your hypocrisy.
You that have so fair parts of woman on you,
Have, too, a woman's heart; which ever yet
Affected eminence, wealth, sovereignty:
Which, to say sooth, are blessings; and which gifts
(Saving your mincing) the capacity
Of your soft cheveril conscience would receive,
If you might please to stretch it.
Anne. Nay, good troth,—
Old Lady. Yes, troth, and troth.—You would not be a queen?
Anne. No, not for all the riches under heaven.
Old Lady. 'Tis strange: a three-pence bow'd would hire me,
Old as I am, to queen it. But, I pray you,
What think you of a duchess? Have you limbs
To bear that load of title?
Anne. No, in truth.
Old Lady. Then you are weakly made. Pluck off a little:
I would not be a young count in your way,
For more than blushing comes to.
Anne. How you do talk!
I swear again, I would not be a queen
For all the world.
Old Lady. In faith, for little England
You'd venture an emballing; I myself
Would for Carnarvonshire, although there long'd
No more to the crown but that.—Lo, who comes here?

Enter the Lord Chamberlain.

Chamberlain. Good morrow, ladies. What were't worth to know
The secret of your conference?
Anne. My good lord,

Not your demand: it values not your asking.
Our mistress' sorrows we were pitying.

Chamberlain. It was a gentle business, and becoming
The action of good women: there is hope
All will be well.

Anne. Now, I pray God, amen!

Chamberlain. You bear a gentle mind, and heavenly blessings
Follow such creatures. That you may, fair lady,
Perceive I speak sincerely, and high note's
Ta'en of your many virtues, the king's majesty
Commends his good opinion to you, and
Does purpose honour to you no less flowing
Than Marchioness of Pembroke; to which title
A thousand pound a year, annual support,
Out of his grace he adds.

Anne. I do not know
What kind of my obedience I should tender:
More than my all is nothing; nor my prayers
Are not words duly hallow'd, nor my wishes
More worth than empty vanities: yet prayers and wishes
Are all I can return. Beseech your lordship,
Vouchsafe to speak my thanks, and my obedience,
As from a blushing handmaid, to his highness;
Whose health and royalty I pray for.

Chamberlain. Lady,
I shall not fail t' approve the fair conceit
The king hath of you.—[*Aside.*] I have perus'd her well:
Beauty and honour in her are so mingled,
That they have caught the king; and who knows yet,
But from this lady may proceed a gem
To lighten all this isle?—[*To her.*] I'll to the king,
And say I spoke with you.

Anne. My honour'd lord.

[*Exit Lord Chamberlain.*

Old Lady. Why, this it is; see, see!
I have been begging sixteen years in court
(Am yet a courtier beggarly), nor could
Come pat betwixt too early and too late,
For any suit of pounds; and you, O fate!
A very fresh-fish here,—fie, fie upon
This compell'd fortune!—have your mouth fill'd up
Before you open it.

Anne. This is strange to me.

Old Lady. How tastes it? is it bitter? forty pence, no.
There was a lady once ('tis an old story)
That would not be a queen, that would she not,
For all the mud in Egypt:—have you heard it?

Anne. Come, you are pleasant.

Old Lady. With your theme I could
O'ermount the lark. The Marchioness of Pembroke!
A thousand pounds a year!—for pure respect;
No other obligation. By my life,
That promises more thousands: honour's train
Is longer than his foreskirt. By this time
I know your back will bear a duchess.—Say,
Are you not stronger than you were?

Anne. Good lady,
Make yourself mirth with your particular fancy,
And leave me out on't. Would I had no being,
If this salute my blood a jot! it faints me
To think what follows.—
The queen is comfortless, and we forgetful
In our long absence. Pray do not deliver
What here you've heard to her.

Old Lady. What do you think me?
[*Exeunt.*

SCENE IV. *A Hall in Black-friars.*

Trumpets, sennet, and cornets. Enter two Vergers, *with short silver wands; next them, two* Scribes, *in the habit of doctors; after them, the* Archbishop of Canterbury *alone; after him, the* Bishops of Lincoln, Ely, Rochester, *and* Saint Asaph; *next them, with some small distance, follows a* Gentleman *bearing the purse, with the great seal, and a cardinal's hat; then two* Priests, *bearing each a silver cross; then a* Gentleman-Usher *bare-headed, accompanied with a* Sergeant-at-Arms, *bearing a silver mace; then two* Gentlemen, *bearing two great silver pillars; after them, side by side, the two* Cardinals WOLSEY *and* CAMPEIUS; *two* Noblemen *with the sword and mace. Then enter the* King *with his Train, followed by the* Queen *with hers. The King takes place under the cloth of state; the two Cardinals sit under him as judges. The Queen takes place at some distance from the King. The Bishops place themselves on each side the court, in manner of a consistory; below them, the Scribes. The Lords sit next the Bishops. The rest of the Attendants stand in convenient order about the stage.*

Wolsey. Whilst our commission from Rome is read,
Let silence be commanded.
King Henry. What's the need?
It hath already publicly been read,
And on all sides th' authority allow'd;
You may, then, spare that time.
Wolsey. Be't so.—Proceed.
Scribe. Say Henry, King of England, come into the court.
Crier. Henry, King of England, come into the court.
King Henry. Here.
Scribe. Say Katherine, Queen of England, come into the court.
Crier. Katherine, Queen of England, come into the court.
[*The Queen makes no answer, rises out of her chair, goes*

about the court, comes to the King, and kneels at his feet; then speaks.

Queen Katherine. Sir, I desire you do me right and justice,
And to bestow your pity on me; for
I am a most poor woman, and a stranger,
Born out of your dominions; having here
No judge indifferent, nor no more assurance
Of equal friendship and proceeding. Alas, sir,
In what have I offended you? what cause
Hath my behaviour given to your displeasure,
That thus you should proceed to put me off,
And take your good grace from me? Heaven witness
I have been to you a true and humble wife,
At all times to your will conformable:
Ever in fear to kindle your dislike,
Yea, subject to your countenance; glad or sorry,
As I saw it inclin'd. When was the hour
I ever contradicted your desire,
Or made it not mine too? Or which of your friends
Have I not strove to love, although I knew
He were mine enemy? what friend of mine,
That had to him deriv'd your anger, did I
Continue in my liking? nay, gave notice
He was from thence discharg'd. Sir, call to mind
That I have been your wife, in this obedience,
Upward of twenty years, and have been blest
With many children by you: if in the course
And process of this time, you can report,
And prove it too, against mine honour aught,
My bond to wedlock, or my love and duty,
Against your sacred person, in God's name,
Turn me away; and let the foul'st contempt
Shut door upon me, and so give me up
To the sharp'st kind of justice. Please you, sir,
The king, your father, was reputed for

A prince most prudent, of an excellent
And unmatch'd wit and judgment: Ferdinand,
My father, King of Spain, was reckon'd one
The wisest prince, that there had reign'd by many
A year before: it is not to be question'd
That they had gather'd a wise council to them
Of every realm, that did debate this business,
Who deem'd our marriage lawful. Wherefore I humbly
Beseech you, sir, to spare me, till I may
Be by my friends in Spain advis'd, whose counsel
I will implore: if not, i' th' name of God,
Your pleasure be fulfill'd!

Wolsey. You have here, lady,
(And of your choice) these reverend fathers; men
Of singular integrity and learning,
Yea, the elect o' th' land, who are assembled
To plead your cause. It shall be therefore bootless,
That longer you desire the court, as well
For your own quiet as to rectify
What is unsettled in the king.

Campeius. His grace
Hath spoken well, and justly: therefore, madam,
It's fit this royal session do proceed,
And that, without delay, their arguments
Be now produc'd and heard.

Queen Katherine. Lord cardinal,
To you I speak.

Wolsey. Your pleasure, madam?

Queen Katherine. Sir,
I am about to weep; but, thinking that
We are a queen (or long have dream'd so), certain
The daughter of a king, my drops of tears
I'll turn to sparks of fire.

Wolsey. Be patient yet.

Queen Katherine. I will, when you are humble; nay, before,

Or God will punish me. I do believe,
Induc'd by potent circumstances, that
You are mine enemy, and make my challenge
You shall not be my judge; for it is you
Have blown this coal betwixt my lord and me,—
Which God's dew quench!—Therefore, I say again,
I utterly abhor, yea, from my soul,
Refuse you for my judge; whom, yet once more,
I hold my most malicious foe, and think not
At all a friend to truth.

Wolsey. I do profess,
You speak not like yourself; who ever yet
Have stood to charity, and display'd th' effects
Of disposition gentle, and of wisdom
O'ertopping woman's power. Madam, you do me wrong:
I have no spleen against you; nor injustice
For you, or any: how far I have proceeded,
Or how far further shall, is warranted
By a commission from the consistory,
Yea, the whole consistory of Rome. You charge me
That I have blown this coal: I do deny it.
The king is present: if it be known to him
That I gainsay my deed, how may he wound,
And worthily, my falsehood! yea, as much
As you have done my truth. If he know
That I am free of your report, he knows
I am not of your wrong: therefore, in him
It lies to cure me; and the cure is, to
Remove these thoughts from you: the which before
His highness shall speak in, I do beseech
You, gracious madam, to unthink your speaking,
And to say so no more.

Queen Katherine. My lord, my lord,
I am a simple woman, much too weak
T' oppose your cunning. You're meek and humble-mouth'd;

You sign your place and calling in full seeming,
With meekness and humility, but your heart
Is cramm'd with arrogancy, spleen, and pride.
You have, by fortune and his highness' favours,
Gone slightly o'er low steps, and now are mounted
Where powers are your retainers; and your words,
Domestics to you, serve your will as't please
Yourself pronounce their office. I must tell you,
You tender more your person's honour than
Your high profession spiritual; that again
I do refuse you for my judge, and here,
Before you all, appeal unto the Pope,
To bring my whole cause 'fore his Holiness,
And to be judg'd by him.
[*She curtsies to the King, and offers to depart.*

Chamberlain. The queen is obstinate,
Stubborn to justice, apt to accuse it, and
Disdainful to be tried by't: 'tis not well.
She's going away.

King Henry. Call her again.

Crier. Katherine, Queen of England, come into the court.

Griffith. Madam, you are call'd back.

Queen Katherine. What need you note it? pray you, keep your way:
When you are call'd, return.—Now the Lord help!
They vex me past my patience.—Pray you, pass on:
I will not tarry; no, nor ever more
Upon this business my appearance make
In any of their courts. [*Exeunt Queen and her Attendants.*

King Henry. Go thy ways, Kate:
That man i' th' world who shall report he has
A better wife, let him in naught be trusted,
For speaking false in that. Thou art, alone
(If thy rare qualities, sweet gentleness,
Thy meekness saint-like, wife-like government,

Obeying in commanding, and thy parts
Sovereign and pious else, could speak thee out),
The queen of earthly queens.—She's noble born;
And, like her true nobility, she has
Carried herself towards me.

Wolsey. Most gracious sir,
In humblest manner I require your highness,
That it shall please you to declare, in hearing
Of all these ears (for where I am robb'd and bound,
There must I be unloos'd, although not there
At once and fully satisfied), whether ever I
Did broach this business to your highness, or
Laid any scruple in your way, which might
Induce you to the question on't? or ever
Have to you, but with thanks to God for such
A royal lady, spake one the least word, that might
Be to the prejudice of her present state,
Or touch of her good person?

King Henry. My lord cardinal,
I do excuse you; yea, upon mine honour,
I free you from't. You are not to be taught
That you have many enemies, that know not
Why they are so, but, like to village curs,
Bark when their fellows do: by some of these
The queen is put in anger. You're excus'd;
But will you be more justified? you ever
Have wish'd the sleeping of this business; never
Desir'd it to be stirr'd; but oft have hinder'd, oft,
The passages made toward it.—On my honour,
I speak my good lord cardinal to this point,
And thus far clear him. Now, what mov'd me to't,
I will be bold with time, and your attention:—
Then, mark th' inducement. Thus it came;—give heed to't.
My conscience first received a tenderness,
Scruple, and prick, on certain speeches uttered

By th' Bishop of Bayonne, then French ambassador;
Who had been hither sent on the debating
A marriage 'twixt the Duke of Orleans and
Our daughter Mary. I' th' progress of this business,
Ere a determinate resolution, he
(I mean the bishop) did require a respite;
Wherein he might the king his lord advertise
Whether our daughter were legitimate,
Respecting this our marriage with the dowager,
Sometimes our brother's wife. This respite shook
The bosom of my conscience, enter'd me,
Yea, with a splitting power, and made to tremble
The region of my breast; which forc'd such way,
That many maz'd considerings did throng,
And press'd in with this caution. First, methought,
This was a judgment on me; that my kingdom,
Well worthy the best heir o' th' world should not
Be gladded in't by me. Then follows, that
I weigh'd the danger which my realms stood in
By this my issue's fail; and that gave to me
Many a groaning throe. Thus hulling in
The wild sea of my conscience, I did steer
Toward this remedy, whereupon we are
Now present here together; that's to say,
I meant to rectify my conscience,—which
I then did feel full sick, and yet not well,—
By all the reverend fathers of the land,
And doctors learn'd. First, I began in private
With you, my Lord of Lincoln: you remember
How under my oppression I did reek
When I first mov'd you.

Lincoln. Very well, my liege.

King Henry. I have spoke long: be pleas'd yourself to say
How far you satisfied me.

Lincoln. So please your highness,

The question did at first so stagger me,—
Bearing a state of mighty moment in't,
And consequence of dread,—that I committed
The daring'st counsel which I had to doubt,
And did entreat your highness to this course
Which you are running here.

King Henry. I then mov'd you,
My Lord of Canterbury; and got your leave
To make this present summons.—Unsolicited
I left no reverend person in this court;
But by particular consent proceeded
Under your hands and seals: therefore, go on;
For no dislike i' th' world against the person
Of the good queen, but the sharp thorny points
Of my alleged reasons drives this forward.
Prove but our marriage lawful,—by my life
And kingly dignity, we are contented
To wear our mortal state to come with her,
Katherine our queen, before the primest creature
That's paragon'd o' th' world.

Campeius. So please your highness,
The queen being absent, 'tis a needful fitness
That we adjourn this court till further day:
Meanwhile must be an earnest motion
Made to the queen, to call back her appeal
She intends unto his Holiness.

King Henry [*Aside*]. I may perceive
These cardinals trifle with me: I abhor
This dilatory sloth and tricks of Rome.
My learn'd and well-beloved servant, Cranmer!
Prithee, return: with thy approach, I know,
My comfort comes along.—Break up the court:
I say, set on. [*Exeunt in manner as they entered.*

PALACE AT BRIDEWELL.

ACT III.

SCENE I. *The Palace at Bridewell. A Room in the Queen's Apartment.*

The Queen *and her* Women *at work.*

Queen Katherine. Take thy lute, wench: my soul grows sad with troubles;
Sing, and disperse 'em, if thou canst. Leave working.

Song.

Orpheus with his lute made trees,
And the mountain-tops that freeze,
Bow themselves when he did sing:
To his music plants and flowers
Ever sprung; as sun and showers
There had made a lasting Spring.

Every thing that heard him play,
Even the billows of the sea,
Hung their heads, and then lay by.
In sweet music is such art,
Killing care and grief of heart
Fall asleep, or, hearing, die.

Enter a Gentleman.

Queen Katherine. How now!

Gentleman. An't please your grace, the two great cardinals
Wait in the presence.

Queen Katherine. Would they speak with me?

Gentleman. They will'd me say so, madam.

Queen Katherine. Pray their graces
To come near. [*Exit Gentleman.*] What can be their business
With me, a poor weak woman, fallen from favour?
I do not like their coming, now I think on't.
They should be good men; their affairs as righteous:
But all hoods make not monks.

Enter WOLSEY *and* CAMPEIUS.

Wolsey. Peace to your highness.

Queen Katherine. Your graces find me here part of a housewife;
I would be all, against the worst may happen.
What are your pleasures with me, reverend lords?

Wolsey. May it please you, noble madam, to withdraw
Into your private chamber, we shall give you
The full cause of our coming.

Queen Katherine. Speak it here.
There's nothing I have done yet, o' my conscience,
Deserves a corner: would all other women
Could speak this with as free a soul as I do!
My lords, I care not (so much I am happy
Above a number) if my actions
Were tried by every tongue, every eye saw 'em
Envy and base opinion set against 'em,
I know my life so even. If your business
Seek me out, and that way I am wife in,
Out with it boldly: truth loves open dealing.

Wolsey. *Tanta est erga te mentis integritas, regina serenissima,—*

Queen Katherine. O, good my lord, no Latin:
I am not such a truant since my coming,
As not to know the language I have liv'd in:
A strange tongue makes my cause more strange, suspicious;
Pray, speak in English. Here are some will thank you,
If you speak truth, for their poor mistress' sake:
Believe me, she has had much wrong. Lord cardinal,
The willing'st sin I ever yet committed
May be absolved in English.

Wolsey. Noble lady,
I am sorry my integrity should breed
(And service to his majesty and you)
So deep suspicion where all faith was meant.
We come not by the way of accusation,
To taint that honour every good tongue blesses,
Nor to betray you any way to sorrow,—
You have too much, good lady; but to know
How you stand minded in the weighty difference
Between the king and you, and to deliver,

Like free and honest men, our just opinions,
And comforts to your cause.
Campeius. Most honour'd madam,
My Lord of York,—out of his noble nature,
Zeal and obedience he still bore your grace,
Forgetting, like a good man, your late censure
Both of his truth and him (which was too far),—
Offers, as I do, in a sign of peace,
His service and his counsel.
Queen Katherine [*Aside*]. To betray me.—
My lords, I thank you both for your good wills;
Ye speak like honest men (pray God ye prove so!),
But how to make ye suddenly an answer,
In such a point of weight so near mine honour
(More near my life, I fear), with my weak wit,
And to such men of gravity and learning,
In truth, I know not. I was set at work
Among my maids; full little, God knows, looking
Either for such men or such business.
For her sake that I have been (for I feel
The last fit of my greatness), good your graces,
Let me have time and counsel for my cause.
Alas, I am a woman, friendless, hopeless!
Wolsey. Madam, you wrong the king's love with these fears:
Your hopes and friends are infinite.
Queen Katherine. In England,
But little for my profit: can you think, lords,
That any Englishman dare give me counsel?
Or be a known friend, 'gainst his highness' pleasure
(Though he be grown so desperate to be honest),
And live a subject? Nay, forsooth, my friends,
They that must weigh out my afflictions,
They that my trust must grow to, live not here:
They are, as all my other comforts, far hence,
In mine own country, lords.

Campeius. I would your grace
Would leave your griefs, and take my counsel.
Queen Katherine. How, sir?
Campeius. Put your main cause into the king's protection;
He's loving and most gracious: 'twill be much
Both for your honour better and your cause;
For if the trial of the law o'ertake ye,
You'll part away disgrac'd.
Wolsey. He tells you rightly.
Queen Katherine. Ye tell me what ye wish for both,—my ruin:
Is this your Christian counsel? out upon ye!
Heaven is above all yet: there sits a Judge
That no king can corrupt.
Campeius. Your rage mistakes us.
Queen Katherine. The more shame for ye! holy men I thought ye,
Upon my soul, two reverend cardinal virtues;
But cardinal sins, and hollow hearts, I fear ye.
Mend 'em for shame, my lords. Is this your comfort?
The cordial that ye bring a wretched lady,—
A woman lost among ye, laugh'd at, scorn'd?
I will not wish ye half my miseries,
I have more charity; but say I warn'd ye:
Take heed, for heaven's sake, take heed, lest at once
The burthen of my sorrows fall upon ye.
Wolsey. Madam, this is a mere distraction;
You turn the good we offer into envy.
Queen Katherine. Ye turn me into nothing. Woe upon ye,
And all such false professors! Would ye have me
(If ye have any justice, any pity,
If ye be any thing but churchmen's habits)
Put my sick cause into his hands that hates me?
Alas, he's banish'd me his bed already;
His love too long ago: I am old, my lords,

And all the fellowship I hold now with him
Is only my obedience. What can happen
To me above this wretchedness? all your studies
Make me a curse like this.

Campeius. Your fears are worse.

Queen Katherine. Have I lived thus long—(let me speak myself,
Since virtue finds no friends)—a wife, a true one?
A woman (I dare say without vain-glory)
Never yet branded with suspicion?
Have I with all my full affections
Still met the king? lov'd him next heaven? obey'd him?
Been, out of fondness, superstitious to him?
Almost forgot my prayers to content him?
And am I thus rewarded? 'Tis not well, lords.
Bring me a constant woman to her husband,
One that ne'er dream'd a joy beyond his pleasure,
And to that woman, when she has done most,
Yet will I add an honour,—a great patience.

Wolsey. Madam, you wander from the good we aim at.

Queen Katherine. My lord, I dare not make myself so guilty,
To give up willingly that noble title
Your master wed me to: nothing but death
Shall e'er divorce my dignities.

Wolsey. Pray hear me.

Queen Katherine. Would I had never trod this English earth,
Or felt the flatteries that grow upon it!
Ye have angels' faces, but heaven knows your hearts!
What will become of me now, wretched lady?
I am the most unhappy woman living.—
Alas, poor wenches, where are now your fortunes?
[*To her Women.*
Shipwrack'd upon a kingdom where no pity,
No friends, no hope, no kindred weep for me
Almost no grave allow'd me.—Like the l

That once was mistress of the field and flourish'd,
I'll hang my head and perish.
Wolsey. If your grace
Could but be brought to know our ends are honest,
You'd feel more comfort. Why should we, good lady,
Upon what cause, wrong you? alas, our places,
The way of our profession is against it:
We are to cure such sorrows, not to sow them.
For goodness' sake, consider what you do;
How you may hurt yourself, ay, utterly
Grow from the king's acquaintance, by this carriage.
The hearts of princes kiss obedience,
So much they love it; but to stubborn spirits,
They swell, and grow as terrible as storms.
I know you have a gentle, noble temper,
A soul as even as a calm: pray think us
Those we profess—peace-makers, friends, and servants.
Campeius. Madam, you'll find it so. You wrong your virtues
With these weak women's fears: a noble spirit
As yours was put into you ever casts
Such doubts, as false coin, from it. The king loves you;
Beware you lose it not: for us, if you please
To trust us in your business, we are ready
To use our utmost studies in your service.
Queen Katherine. Do what ye will, my lords, and pray forgive me,
If I have us'd myself unmannerly.
You know I am a woman, lacking wit
To make a seemly answer to such persons.
Pray do my service to his majesty:
He has my heart yet, and shall have my prayers,
While I shall have my life. Come, reverend fathers;
Bestow your counsels on me: she now begs
That little thought, when she set footing here,
She should have bought her dignities so dear. [*Exeunt.*

SCENE II. *Ante-chamber to the King's Apartment.*

Enter the DUKE OF NORFOLK, *the* DUKE OF SUFFOLK, *the* EARL OF SURREY, *and the* Lord Chamberlain.

Norfolk. If you will now unite in your complaints,
And force them with a constancy, the cardinal
Cannot stand under them: if you omit
The offer of this time, I cannot promise
But that you shall sustain more new disgraces,
With these you bear already.

Surrey. I am joyful
To meet the least occasion that may give me
Remembrance of my father-in-law, the duke,
To be reveng'd on him.

Suffolk. Which of the peers
Have uncontemn'd gone by him, or at least
Strangely neglected? When did he regard
The stamp of nobleness in any person,
Out of himself?

Chamberlain. My lords, you speak your pleasures.
What he deserves of you and me, I know;
What we can do to him (though now the time
Gives way to us), I much fear. If you cannot
Bar his access to th' king, never attempt
Any thing on him, for he hath a witchcraft
Over the king in 's tongue.

Norfolk. O, fear him not;
His spell in that is out: the king hath found
Matter against him that for ever mars
The honey of his language. No, he's settled,
Not to come off, in his displeasure.

Surrey. Sir,
I should be glad to hear such news as this
Once every hour.

Norfolk. Believe it, this is true.

In the divorce, his contrary proceedings
Are all unfolded; wherein he appears,
As I could wish mine enemy.
Surrey. How came
His practices to light?
Suffolk. Most strangely.
Surrey. O, how? how?
Suffolk. The cardinal's letter to the Pope miscarried,
And came to th' eye o' th' king; wherein was read,
How that the cardinal did entreat his Holiness
To stay the judgment o' th' divorce; for if
It did take place, "I do," quoth he, "perceive
My king is tangled in affection to
A creature of the queen's, Lady Anne Bullen."
Surrey. Has the king this?
Suffolk. Believe it.
Surrey. Will this work?
Chamberlain. The king in this perceives him, how he coasts
And hedges his own way. But in this point
All his tricks founder, and he brings his physic
After his patient's death: the king already
Hath married the fair lady.
Surrey. Would he had!
Suffolk. May you be happy in your wish, my lord;
For, I profess, you have it.
Surrey. Now all my joy
Trace the conjunction!
Suffolk. My amen to't.
Norfolk. All men's.
Suffolk. There's order given for her coronation:
Marry, this is yet but young, and may be left
To some ears unrecounted.—But, my lords,
She is a gallant creature, and complete
In mind and feature: I persuade me, from her

Will fall some blessing to this land, which shall
In it be memoriz'd.

Surrey. But will the king
Digest this letter of the cardinal's?
The Lord forbid!

Norfolk. Marry, amen!

Suffolk. No, no:
There be more wasps that buzz about his nose
Will make this sting the sooner. Cardinal Campeius
Is stolen away to Rome; hath ta'en no leave;
Has left the cause o' th' king unhandled, and
Is posted, as the agent of our cardinal,
To second all his plot. I do assure you,
The king cried "ha!" at this.

Chamberlain. Now God incense him,
And let him cry "ha!" louder.

Norfolk. But, my lord,
When returns Cranmer?

Suffolk. He is return'd in his opinions, which
Have satisfied the king for his divorce,
Together with all famous colleges
Almost in Christendom. Shortly, I believe,
His second marriage shall be publish'd, and
Her coronation. Katherine no more
Shall be call'd queen, but princess dowager,
And widow to Prince Arthur.

Norfolk. This same Cranmer's
A worthy fellow, and hath ta'en much pain
In the king's business.

Suffolk. He has; and we shall see him
For it an archbishop.

Norfolk. So I hear.

Suffolk. 'Tis so.
The cardinal—

Enter WOLSEY *and* CROMWELL.

Norfolk. Observe, observe; he's moody.
Wolsey. The packet, Cromwell,
Gave't you the king?
Cromwell. To his own hand, in 's bedchamber.
Wolsey. Look'd he o' th' inside of the paper?
Cromwell. Presently
He did unseal them, and the first he view'd,
He did it with a serious mind; a heed
Was in his countenance; you he bade
Attend him here this morning.
Wolsey. Is he ready
To come abroad?
Cromwell. I think by this he is.
Wolsey. Leave me a while.— [*Exit Cromwell.*
It shall be to the Duchess of Alençon,
The French king's sister: he shall marry her.—
Anne Bullen? No; I'll no Anne Bullens for him:
There's more in't than fair visage.—Bullen!
No, we'll no Bullens.—Speedily I wish
To hear from Rome.—The Marchioness of Pembroke!
Norfolk. He's discontented.
Suffolk. May be he hears the king
Does whet his anger to him.
Surrey. Sharp enough,
Lord, for thy justice!
Wolsey. The late queen's gentlewoman, a knight's daughter,
To be her mistress' mistress! the queen's queen!—
This candle burns not clear: 'tis I must snuff it;
Then out it goes.—What though I know her virtuous,
And well deserving, yet I know her for
A spleeny Lutheran; and not wholesome to
Our cause, that she should lie i' th' bosom of
Our hard-rul'd king. Again, there is sprung up

An heretic, an arch one, Cranmer; one
Hath crawl'd into the favour of the king,
And is his oracle.

Norfolk. He is vex'd at something.

Suffolk. I would 'twere something that would fret the string,
The master-cord on 's heart!

Enter the King, *reading a schedule; and* LOVELL.

Suffolk. The king, the king.

King Henry. What piles of wealth hath he accumulated
To his own portion! and what expense by the hour
Seems to flow from him! How, i' th' name of thrift,
Does he rake this together?—Now, my lords,—
Saw you the cardinal?

Norfolk. My lord, we have
Stood here observing him. Some strange commotion
Is in his brain: he bites his lip, and starts;
Stops on a sudden, looks upon the ground,
Then lays his finger on his temple; straight
Springs out into fast gait; then stops again,
Strikes his breast hard; and anon he casts
His eye against the moon. In most strange postures
We have seen him set himself.

King Henry. It may well be:
There is a mutiny in 's mind. This morning
Papers of state he sent me to peruse,
As I requir'd; and wot you what I found
There,—on my conscience, put unwittingly?
Forsooth, an inventory, thus importing,—
The several parcels of his plate, his treasure,
Rich stuffs, and ornaments of household, which
I find at such proud rate, that it out-speaks
Possession of a subject.

Norfolk. It's heaven's will:

Some spirit put this paper in the packet,
To bless your eye withal.
King Henry. If we did think
His contemplation were above the earth,
And fix'd on spiritual object, he should still
Dwell in his musings; but I am afraid
His thinkings are below the moon, not worth
His serious considering.
[*He takes his seat, and whispers Lovell, who goes to Wolsey.*
Wolsey. Heaven forgive me!
Ever God bless your highness!
King Henry. Good my lord,
You are full of heavenly stuff, and bear the inventory
Of your best graces in your mind, the which
You were now running o'er: you have scarce time
To steal from spiritual leisure a brief span,
To keep your earthly audit. Sure, in that
I deem you an ill husband, and am glad
To have you therein my companion.
Wolsey. Sir,
For holy offices I have a time; a time
To think upon the part of business which
I bear i' th' state; and nature does require
Her times of preservation, which, perforce,
I her frail son, amongst my brethren mortal,
Must give my tendance to.
King Henry. You have said well.
Wolsey. And ever may your highness yoke together,
As I will lend you cause, my doing well
With my well saying!
King Henry. 'Tis well said again;
And 'tis a kind of good deed to say well:
And yet words are no deeds. My father lov'd you;
He said he did, and with his deed did crown
His word upon you: since I had my office,

I have kept you next my heart; have not alone
Employ'd you where high profits might come home,
But par'd my present havings, to bestow
My bounties upon you.

Wolsey. What should this mean?

Surrey [*Aside*]. The Lord increase this business!

King Henry. Have I not made you
The prime man of the state? I pray you, tell me,
If what I now pronounce you have found true;
And, if you may confess it, say withal,
If you are bound to us or no. What say you?

Wolsey. My sovereign, I confess, your royal graces,
Shower'd on me daily, have been more than could
My studied purposes requite; which went
Beyond all man's endeavours; my endeavours
Have ever come too short of my desires,
Yet fil'd with my abilities. Mine own ends
Have been mine so, that evermore they pointed
To th' good of your most sacred person and
The profit of the state. For your great graces
Heap'd upon me, poor undeserver, I
Can nothing render but allegiant thanks;
My prayers to heaven for you; my loyalty,
Which ever has, and ever shall be growing,
Till death, that winter, kill it.

King Kenry. Fairly answer'd:
A loyal and obedient subject is
Therein illustrated. The honour of it
Does pay the act of it; as, i' th' contrary,
The foulness is the punishment. I presume,
That as my hand has open'd bounty to you,
My heart dropp'd love, my power rain'd honour, more
On you than any; so your hand, and heart,
Your brain, and every function of your power,
Should, notwithstanding that your bond of duty,

As 'twere in love's particular, be more
To me, your friend, than any.

Wolsey. I do profess,
That for your highness' good I ever labour'd
More than mine own; that am true, and will be,
Though all the world should crack their duty to you,
And throw it from their soul. Though perils did
Abound as thick as thought could make them, and
Appear in forms more horrid, yet my duty
(As doth a rock against the chiding flood)
Should the approach of this wild river break,
And stand unshaken yours.

King Henry. 'Tis nobly spoken.
Take notice, lords, he has a loyal breast,
For you have seen him open't.—Read o'er this:
[*Giving him papers.*
And, after, this; and then to breakfast, with
What appetite you have.

[*Exit King, frowning upon Cardinal Wolsey: the Nobles throng after him, smiling and whispering.*

Wolsey. What should this mean?
What sudden anger's this? how have I reap'd it?
He parted frowning from me, as if ruin
Leap'd from his eyes: so looks the chafed lion
Upon the daring huntsman that has gall'd him,
Then makes him nothing. I must read this paper;
I fear, the story of his anger.—'Tis so:
This paper has undone me!—'Tis th' account
Of all that world of wealth I have drawn together
For mine own ends; indeed, to gain the Popedom,
And fee my friends in Rome. O negligence,
Fit for a fool to fall by! What cross devil
Made me put this main secret in the packet
I sent the king? Is there no way to cure this?
No new device to beat this from his brains?

I know 'twill stir him strongly; yet I know
A way, if it take right, in spite of fortune
Will bring me off again. What's this?—"To the Pope?"
The letter, as I live, with all the business
I writ to 's Holiness. Nay then, farewell!
I have touch'd the highest point of all my greatness,
And from that full meridian of my glory,
I haste now to my setting: I shall fall
Like a bright exhalation in the evening,
And no man see me more.

Enter the DUKES OF NORFOLK *and* SUFFOLK, *the* EARL OF SURREY, *and the* Lord Chamberlain.

Norfolk. Hear the king's pleasure, cardinal; who commands you
To render up the great seal presently
Into our hands, and to confine yourself
To Asher-house, my Lord of Winchester's,
Till you hear further from his highness.
Wolsey. Stay:
Where's your commission, lords? words cannot carry
Authority so weighty.
Suffolk. Who dare cross 'em,
Bearing the king's will from his mouth expressly?
Wolsey. Till I find more than will, or words, to do it
(I mean your malice), know, officious lords,
I dare and must deny it. Now, I feel
Of what coarse metal ye are moulded—envy.
How eagerly ye follow my disgraces,
As if it fed ye! and how sleek and wanton
Ye appear in every thing may bring my ruin!
Follow your envious courses, men of malice;
You have Christian warrant for 'em, and, no doubt,
In time will find their fit rewards. That seal
You ask with such a violence, the king

(Mine and your master) with his own hand gave me;
Bade me enjoy it, with the place and honours,
During my life, and to confirm his goodness,
Tied it by letters patents. Now, who'll take it?
Surrey. The king that gave it.
Wolsey. It must be himself, then.
Surrey. Thou art a proud traitor, priest.
Wolsey. Proud lord, thou liest:
Within these forty hours Surrey durst better
Have burnt that tongue than said so.
Surrey. Thy ambition,
Thou scarlet sin, robb'd this bewailing land
Of noble Buckingham, my father-in-law:
The heads of all thy brother cardinals,
With thee and all thy best parts bound together,
Weigh'd not a hair of his. Plague of your policy!
You sent me deputy for Ireland,
Far from his succour, from the king, from all
That might have mercy on the fault thou gav'st him;
Whilst your great goodness, out of holy pity,
Absolv'd him with an axe.
Wolsey. This, and all else
This talking lord can lay upon my credit,
I answer, is most false. The duke by law
Found his deserts: how innocent I was
From any private malice in his end,
His noble jury and foul cause can witness.
If I lov'd many words, lord, I should tell you
You have as little honesty as honour,
That in the way of loyalty and truth
Toward the king, my ever royal master,
Dare mate a sounder man than Surrey can be,
And all that love his follies.
Surrey. By my soul,
Your long coat, priest, protects you: thou shouldst feel

My sword i' th' life-blood of thee else.—My lords,
Can ye endure to hear this arrogance?
And from this fellow? If we live thus tamely,
To be thus jaded by a piece of scarlet,
Farewell nobility; let his grace go forward,
And dare us with his cap, like larks.

Wolsey. All goodness
Is poison to thy stomach.

Surrey. Yes, that goodness
Of gleaning all the land's wealth into one,
Into your own hands, cardinal, by extortion;
The goodness of your intercepted packets,
You writ to th' Pope against the king; your goodness,
Since you provoke me, shall be most notorious.—
My Lord of Norfolk, as you are truly noble,
As you respect the common good, the state
Of our despis'd nobility, our issues
(Who, if he live, will scarce be gentlemen),
Produce the grand sum of his sins, the articles
Collected from his life:—I'll startle you.

Wolsey. How much, methinks, I could despise this man,
But that I am bound in charity against it.

Norfolk. Those articles, my lord, are in the king's hand;
But, thus much, they are foul ones.

Wolsey. So much fairer
And spotless shall mine innocence arise
When the king knows my truth.

Surrey. This cannot save you.
I thank my memory, I yet remember
Some of these articles; and out they shall.
Now, if you can blush and cry guilty, cardinal,
You'll shew a little honesty.

Wolsey. Speak on, sir;
I dare your worst objections: if I blush,
It is to see a nobleman want manners.

Surrey. I had rather want those than my head. Have at you.
First, that without the king's assent or knowledge,
You wrought to be a legate; by which power
You maim'd the jurisdiction of all bishops.

Norfolk. Then, that in all you writ to Rome, or else
To foreign princes, *Ego et Rex meus*
Was still inscrib'd; in which you brought the king
To be your servant.

Suffolk. Then, that without the knowledge
Either of king or council, when you went
Ambassador to the emperor, you made bold
To carry into Flanders the great seal.

Surrey. Item, you sent a large commission
To Gregory de Cassalis, to conclude,
Without the king's will or the state's allowance,
A league between his highness and Ferrara.

Suffolk. That out of mere ambition you have caus'd
Your holy hat to be stamp'd on the king's coin.

Surrey. Then, that you have sent innumerable substance
(By what means got, I leave to your own conscience)
To furnish Rome, and to prepare the ways
You have for dignities; to the mere undoing
Of all the kingdom. Many more there are;
Which, since they are of you, and odious,
I will not taint my mouth with.

Chamberlain. O, my lord,
Press not a falling man too far! 'tis virtue.
His faults lie open to the laws: let them,
Not you, correct him. My heart weeps to see him
So little of his great self.

Surrey. I forgive him.

Suffolk. Lord cardinal, the king's further pleasure is,—
Because all those things you have done of late
By your power legatine within this kingdom,

Fall into th' compass of a *præmunire*,—
That therefore such a writ be sued against you:
To forfeit all your goods, lands, tenements,
Chattels, and whatsoever, and to be
Out of the king's protection.—This is my charge.

Norfolk. And so we'll leave you to your meditations
How to live better. For your stubborn answer,
About the giving back the great seal to us,
The king shall know it, and, no doubt, shall thank you.
So, fare you well, my little good lord cardinal.
[*Exeunt all but Wolsey.*

Wolsey. So, farewell to the little good you bear me.
Farewell, a long farewell, to all my greatness!
This is the state of man: to-day he puts forth
The tender leaves of hopes; to-morrow blossoms,
And bears his blushing honours thick upon him;
The third day comes a frost, a killing frost,
And,—when he thinks, good easy man, full surely
His greatness is a ripening,—nips his root,
And then he falls as I do. I have ventur'd,
Like little wanton boys that swim on bladders,
This many summers in a sea of glory,
But far beyond my depth: my high-blown pride
At length broke under me, and now has left me
Weary and old with service, to the mercy
Of a rude stream, that must for ever hide me.
Vain pomp and glory of this world, I hate ye:
I feel my heart new open'd. O, how wretched
Is that poor man, that hangs on princes' favours!
There is betwixt that smile we would aspire to,
That sweet aspect of princes and their ruin,
More pangs and fears than wars or women have;
And when he falls, he falls like Lucifer,—
Never to hope again.—

Enter CROMWELL, *amazedly.*

Why, how now, Cromwell!

Cromwell. I have no power to speak, sir.

Wolsey. What! amaz'd
At my misfortunes? can thy spirit wonder
A great man should decline? Nay, an you weep,
I am fallen indeed.

Cromwell. How does your grace?

Wolsey. Why, well:
Never so truly happy, my good Cromwell.
I know myself now; and I feel within me
A peace above all earthly dignities,
A still and quiet conscience. The king has cur'd me,
I humbly thank his grace, and from these shoulders,
These ruin'd pillars, out of pity, taken
A load would sink a navy—too much honour.
O, 'tis a burthen, Cromwell, 'tis a burthen
Too heavy for a man that hopes for heaven.

Cromwell. I am glad your grace has made that right use of it.

Wolsey. I hope I have: I am able now, methinks
(Out of a fortitude of soul I feel),
To endure more miseries, and greater far,
Than my weak-hearted enemies dare offer.
What news abroad?

Cromwell. The heaviest and the worst
Is your displeasure with the king.

Wolsey. God bless him!

Cromwell. The next is, that Sir Thomas More is chosen
Lord Chancellor in your place.

Wolsey. That's somewhat sudden:
But he's a learned man. May he continue
Long in his highness' favour, and do justice
For truth's sake, and his conscience; that his bones,

When he has run his course, and sleeps in blessings,
May have a tomb of orphans' tears wept on 'em!
What more?

Cromwell. That Cranmer is return'd with welcome,
Install'd Lord Archbishop of Canterbury.

Wolsey. That's news indeed!

Cromwell. Last, that the Lady Anne,
Whom the king hath in secrecy long married,
This day was view'd in open as his queen,
Going to chapel; and the voice is now
Only about her coronation.

Wolsey. There was the weight that pull'd me down. O Cromwell!
The king has gone beyond me: all my glories
In that one woman I have lost for ever.
No sun shall ever usher forth mine honours,
Or gild again the noble troops that waited
Upon my smiles. Go, get thee from me, Cromwell;
I am a poor fallen man, unworthy now
To be thy lord and master. Seek the king:
That sun, I pray, may never set! I have told him
What and how true thou art: he will advance thee.
Some little memory of me will stir him
(I know his noble nature) not to let
Thy hopeful service perish too. Good Cromwell,
Neglect him not; make use now, and provide
For thine own future safety.

Cromwell. O my lord!
Must I then leave you? must I needs forego
So good, so noble, and so true a master?
Bear witness, all that have not hearts of iron,
With what a sorrow Cromwell leaves his lord!—
The king shall have my service; but my prayers
For ever and for ever shall be yours.

Wolsey. Cromwell, I did not think to shed a tear

In all my miseries; but thou hast forc'd me,
Out of thy honest truth, to play the woman.
Let's dry our eyes; and thus far hear me, Cromwell:
And,—when I am forgotten, as I shall be,
And sleep in dull, cold marble, where no mention
Of me more must be heard of,—say, I taught thee;
Say, Wolsey, that once trod the ways of glory,
And sounded all the depths and shoals of honour,
Found thee a way, out of his wrack, to rise in;
A sure and safe one, though thy master miss'd it.
Mark but my fall, and that that ruin'd me.
Cromwell, I charge thee, fling away ambition:
By that sin fell the angels; how can man, then,
The image of his Maker, hope to win by't?
Love thyself last: cherish those hearts that hate thee:
Corruption wins not more than honesty.
Still in thy right hand carry gentle peace,
To silence envious tongues: be just, and fear not.
Let all the ends thou aim'st at be thy country's,
Thy God's, and truth's: then, if thou fall'st, O Cromwell!
Thou fall'st a blessed martyr. Serve the king;
And,—prithee, lead me in:
There take an inventory of all I have,
To the last penny; 'tis the king's: my robe,
And my integrity to heaven, is all
I dare now call mine own. O Cromwell, Cromwell!
Had I but serv'd my God with half the zeal
I serv'd my king, he would not in mine age
Have left me naked to mine enemies.

Cromwell. Good sir, have patience.

Wolsey. So I have. Farewell
The hopes of court! my hopes in heaven do dwell. [*Exeunt.*

ACT IV.

SCENE I. *A Street in Westminster.*

Enter two Gentlemen, *meeting.*

1 *Gentleman.* You're well met, once again.

2 *Gentleman.* So are you.
1 *Gentleman.* You come to take your stand here, and behold
The Lady Anne pass from her coronation?
2 *Gentleman.* 'Tis all my business. At our last encounter,
The Duke of Buckingham came from his trial.
1 *Gentleman.* 'Tis very true; but that time offer'd sorrow;
This, general joy.
2 *Gentleman.* 'Tis well: the citizens,
I am sure, have shown at full their royal minds—
As, let 'em have their rights, they are ever forward—
In celebration of this day with shows,
Pageants, and sights of honour.
1 *Gentleman.* Never greater;
Nor, I'll assure you, better taken, sir.
2 *Gentleman.* May I be bold to ask what that contains,
That paper in your hand?
1 *Gentleman.* Yes; 'tis the list
Of those that claim their offices this day,
By custom of the coronation.
The Duke of Suffolk is the first, and claims
To be high-steward: next, the Duke of Norfolk,
He to be earl marshal. You may read the rest.
2 *Gentleman.* I thank you, sir: had I not known those customs,
I should have been beholding to your paper.
But, I beseech you, what's become of Katherine,
The princess dowager? how goes her business?
1 *Gentleman.* That I can tell you too. The Archbishop
Of Canterbury, accompanied with other
Learned and reverend fathers of his order,
Held a late court at Dunstable, six miles off
From Ampthill, where the princess lay; to which
She was often cited by them, but appear'd not:
And, to be short, for not appearance, and
The king's late scruple, by the main assent

Of all these learned men she was divorc'd,
And the late marriage made of none effect:
Since which she was remov'd to Kimbolton,
Where she remains now, sick.

2 *Gentleman.* Alas, good lady!—
[*Trumpets.*
The trumpets sound: stand close, the queen is coming.
[*Hautboys.*

The Order of the Procession.

A lively flourish of trumpets: then Enter

1. *Two* Judges.
2. Lord Chancellor, *with purse and mace before him.*
3. Choristers *singing.*
4. Mayor of London, *bearing the mace. Then,* Garter, *in his coat of arms; and on his head a gilt copper crown.*
5. MARQUESS DORSET, *bearing a sceptre of gold; on his head a demi-coronal of gold. With him the* EARL OF SURREY, *bearing the rod of silver with the dove; crowned with an earl's coronet. Collars of SS.*
6. DUKE OF SUFFOLK, *in his robe of estate, his coronet on his head, bearing a long white wand, as High-steward. With him, the* DUKE OF NORFOLK, *with the rod of marshalship; a coronet on his head. Collars of SS.*
7. *A canopy borne by four of the* Cinque-ports; *under it, the* Queen *in her robe; her hair richly adorned with pearl; crowned. On each side her, the* Bishops of London *and* Winchester.
8. *The old* DUCHESS OF NORFOLK, *in a coronal of gold, wrought with flowers, bearing the* Queen's *train.*
9. *Certain* Ladies *or* Countesses, *with plain circlets of gold, without flowers.*

2 *Gentleman.* A royal train, believe me.—These I know:
Who's that, that bears the sceptre?

1 *Gentleman.* Marquess Dorset:
And that the Earl of Surrey, with the rod.

2 *Gentleman.* A bold, brave gentleman. That should be
The Duke of Suffolk.

1 *Gentleman.* 'Tis the same; high-steward.

2 *Gentleman.* And that my Lord of Norfolk?

1 *Gentleman.* Yes.

2 *Gentleman.* Heaven bless thee!
[*Looking on the Queen.*
Thou hast the sweetest face I ever look'd on.—
Sir, as I have a soul, she is an angel.

1 *Gentleman.* They that bear
The cloth of honour over her, are four barons
Of the Cinque-ports.

2 *Gentleman.* Those men are happy; and so are all are near her.
I take it she that carries up the train
Is that old noble lady, Duchess of Norfolk.

1 *Gentleman.* It is; and all the rest are countesses.

2 *Gentleman.* Their coronets say so. These are stars, indeed.
[*Exit Procession, with a great flourish of trumpets.*

Enter a third Gentleman.

1 *Gentleman.* God save you, sir! Where have you been broiling?

3 *Gentleman.* Among the crowd i' th' abbey; where a finger
Could not be wedg'd in more: I am stifled
With the mere rankness of their joy.

2 *Gentleman.* You saw the ceremony?

3 *Gentleman.* That I did.

1 *Gentleman.* How was it?

3 *Gentleman.* Well worth the seeing.

2 *Gentleman.* Good sir, speak it to us.

3 *Gentleman.* As well as I am able. The rich stream

Of lords and ladies, having brought the queen
To a prepar'd place in the choir, fell off
A distance from her; while her grace sat down
To rest a while,—some half an hour or so,—
In a rich chair of state, opposing freely
The beauty of her person to the people.
Believe me, sir, she is the goodliest woman
That ever lay by man: which when the people
Had the full view of, such a noise arose
As the shrouds make at sea in a stiff tempest,
As loud and to as many tunes: hats, cloaks
(Doublets, I think), flew up; and had their faces
Been loose, this day they had been lost. Such joy
I never saw before. No man living
Could say, "This is my wife," there; all were woven
So strangely in one piece.

2 *Gentleman.* But what follow'd?

3 *Gentleman.* At length her grace rose, and with modest paces
Came to the altar; where she kneel'd, and saint-like
Cast her fair eyes to heaven, and pray'd devoutly:
Then rose again, and bow'd her to the people:
When by the Archbishop of Canterbury
She had all the royal makings of a queen;
As holy oil, Edward Confessor's crown,
The rod, and bird of peace, and all such emblems
Laid nobly on her; which perform'd, the choir,
With all the choicest music of the kingdom,
Together sung *Te Deum.* So she parted,
And with the same full state pac'd back again
To York-place, where the feast is held.

1 *Gentleman.* Sir,
You must no more call it York-place; that's past;
For, since the cardinal fell, that title's lost:
'Tis now the king's, and call'd Whitehall.

3 *Gentleman.* I know it;
But 'tis so lately alter'd, that the old name
Is fresh about me.

2 *Gentleman.* What two reverend bishops
Were those that went on each side of the queen?

3 *Gentleman.* Stokesly and Gardiner; the one of Win- [chester,
Newly preferr'd from the king's secretary;
The other, London.

2 *Gentleman.* He of Winchester
Is held no great good lover of the archbishop's,
The virtuous Cranmer.

3 *Gentleman.* All the land knows that:
However, yet there's no great breach; when it comes,
Cranmer will find a friend will not shrink from him.

2 *Gentleman.* Who may that be, I pray you?

3 *Gentleman.* Thomas Cromwell;
A man in much esteem with th' king, and truly
A worthy friend.—The king has made him
Master o' th' jewel-house,
And one, already, of the privy-council.

2 *Gentleman.* He will deserve more.

3 *Gentleman.* Yes, without all doubt.
Come, gentlemen, ye shall go my way, which
Is to the court; and there ye shall be my guests:
Something I can command. As I walk thither,
I'll tell ye more.

Both. You may command us, sir. [*Exeunt.*

SCENE II. *Kimbolton.*

Enter KATHERINE, *dowager, sick; led between* GRIFFITH *and* PATIENCE.

Griffith. How does your grace?

Katherine. O, Griffith, sick to death:
My legs, like loaden branches, bow to th' earth,

Willing to leave their burthen. Reach a chair :—
So,—now, methinks, I feel a little ease.
Didst thou not tell me, Griffith, as thou ledd'st me,
That the great child of honour, Cardinal Wolsey,
Was dead?

Griffith. Yes, madam ; but I think your grace,
Out of the pain you suffer'd, gave no ear to't.

Katherine. Prithee, good Griffith, tell me how he died :
If well, he stepp'd before me, happily,
For my example.

Griffith. Well, the voice goes, madam :
For after the stout Earl Northumberland
Arrested him at York, and brought him forward,
As a man sorely tainted, to his answer,
He fell sick suddenly, and grew so ill,
He could not sit his mule.

Katherine. Alas, poor man!

Griffith. At last, with easy roads, he came to Leicester ;
Lodg'd in the abbey, where the reverend abbot,
With all his covent, honourably receiv'd him :
To whom he gave these words,—"O father abbot,
An old man, broken with the storms of state,
Is come to lay his weary bones among ye ;
Give him a little earth for charity!"
So went to bed, where eagerly his sickness
Pursu'd him still ; and three nights after this,
About the hour of eight, which he himself
Foretold should be his last, full of repentance,
Continual meditations, tears, and sorrows,
He gave his honours to the world again,
His blessed part to heaven, and slept in peace.

Katherine. So may he rest! his faults lie gently on him!
Yet thus far, Griffith, give me leave to speak him,
And yet with charity.—He was a man
Of an unbounded stomach, ever ranking

Himself with princes ; one that by suggestion
Tith'd all the kingdom : simony was fair play ;
His own opinion was his law : i' th' presence
He would say untruths, and be ever double,
Both in his words and meaning. He was never,
But where he meant to ruin, pitiful :
His promises were, as he then was, mighty ;
But his performance, as he is now, nothing.
Of his own body he was ill, and gave
The clergy ill example.

Griffith. Noble madam,
Men's evil manners live in brass ; their virtues
We write in water. May it please your highness
To hear me speak his good now?

Katherine. Yes, good Griffith ;
I were malicious else.

Griffith. This cardinal,
Though from an humble stock, undoubtedly
Was fashion'd to much honour from his cradle.
He was a scholar, and a ripe and good one ;
Exceeding wise, fair spoken, and persuading :
Lofty and sour to them that lov'd him not ;
But to those men that sought him, sweet as summer :
And though he were unsatisfied in getting
(Which was a sin), yet in bestowing, madam,
He was most princely. Ever witness for him
Those twins of learning that he rais'd in you,
Ipswich and Oxford ; one of which fell with him,
Unwilling to outlive the good that did it ;
The other, though unfinish'd, yet so famous,
So excellent in art, and still so rising,
That Christendom shall ever speak his virtue.
His overthrow heap'd happiness upon him ;
For then, and not till then, he felt himself,
And found the blessedness of being little :

And, to add greater honours to his age
Than man could give him, he died fearing God.
Katherine. After my death I wish no other herald,
No other speaker of my living actions,
To keep mine honour from corruption,
But such an honest chronicler as Griffith.
Whom I most hated living, thou hast made me,
With thy religious truth and modesty,
Now in his ashes honour. Peace be with him !—
Patience, be near me still ; and set me lower :
I have not long to trouble thee.—Good Griffith,
Cause the musicians play me that sad note
I nam'd my knell, whilst I sit meditating
On that celestial harmony I go to. [*Sad and solemn music.*
Griffith. She is asleep. Good wench, let's sit down quiet,
For fear we wake her :—softly, gentle Patience.

The Vision.

Enter, solemnly tripping one after another, six Personages, clad in white robes, wearing on their heads garlands of bays, and golden vizards on their faces ; branches of bays, or palm, in their hands. They first congee unto her, then dance ; and, at certain changes, the first two hold a spare garland over her head ; at which the other four make reverend curtsies ; then, the two that held the garland deliver the same to the other next two, who observe the same order in their changes, and holding the garland over her head. Which done, they deliver the same garland to the last two, who likewise observe the same order : at which (as it were by inspiration) she makes in her sleep signs of rejoicing, and holdeth up her hands to heaven. And so in their dancing they vanish, carrying the garland with them. The music continues.

Katherine. Spirits of peace, where are ye ? Are ye all gone,
And leave me here in wretchedness behind ye ?

Griffith. Madam, we are here.
Katherine. It is not you I call for.
Saw ye none enter since I slept?
Griffith. None, madam.
Katherine. No! Saw you not, even now, a blessed troop
Invite me to a banquet, whose bright faces
Cast thousand beams upon me like the sun?
They promis'd me eternal happiness,
And brought me garlands, Griffith, which I feel
I am not worthy yet to wear: I shall, assuredly.
Griffith. I am most joyful, madam, such good dreams
Possess your fancy.
Katherine. Bid the music leave;
They are harsh and heavy to me. [*Music ceases.*
Patience. Do you note
How much her grace is alter'd on the sudden?
How long her face is drawn! How pale she looks,
And of an earthy cold! Mark her eyes!
Griffith. She is going, wench. Pray, pray.
Patience. Heaven comfort her!

Enter a Messenger.

Messenger. An't like your grace,—
Katherine. You are a saucy fellow:
Deserve we no more reverence?
Griffith. You are to blame,
Knowing she will not lose her wonted greatness,
To use so rude behaviour: go to; kneel.
Messenger. I humbly do entreat your highness' pardon;
My haste made me unmannerly. There is staying
A gentleman sent from the king to see you.
Katherine. Admit him entrance, Griffith: but this fellow
Let me ne'er see again. [*Exeunt Griffith and Messenger.*

Enter GRIFFITH, *with* CAPUCIUS.

If my sight fail not,
You should be lord ambassador from the emperor,
My royal nephew; and your name Capucius.
Capucius. Madam, the same, your servant.
Katherine. O, my lord,
The times and titles now are alter'd strangely
With me since first you knew me! But, I pray you,
What is your pleasure with me?
Capucius. Noble lady,
First, mine own service to your grace; the next,
The king's request that I would visit you;
Who grieves much for your weakness, and by me
Sends you his princely commendations,
And heartily entreats you take good comfort.
Katherine. O, my good lord, that comfort comes too late:
'Tis like a pardon after execution.
That gentle physic, given in time, had cur'd me;
But now I am past all comforts here but prayers.
How does his highness?
Capucius. Madam, in good health.
Katherine. So may he ever do; and ever flourish,
When I shall dwell with worms, and my poor name
Banish'd the kingdom.—Patience, is that letter
I caus'd you write yet sent away?
Patience. No, madam.
[*Giving it to Katherine.*
Katherine. Sir, I most humbly pray you to deliver
This to my lord the king,—
Capucius. Most willing, madam.
Katherine. In which I have commended to his goodness
The model of our chaste loves, his young daughter
(The dews of heaven fall thick in blessings on her!);
Beseeching him to give her virtuous breeding

(She is young, and of a noble modest nature,—
I hope, she will deserve well), and a little
To love her for her mother's sake, that lov'd him,
Heaven knows how dearly! My next poor petition
Is, that his noble grace would have some pity
Upon my wretched women, that so long
Have follow'd both my fortunes faithfully:
Of which there is not one, I dare avow
(And now I should not lie), but will deserve,
For virtue and true beauty of the soul,
For honesty and decent carriage,
A right good husband, let him be a noble;
And, sure, those men are happy that shall have 'em.
The last is for my men:—they are the poorest,
But poverty could never draw 'em from me;—
That they may have their wages duly paid 'em,
And something over to remember me by:
If heaven had pleas'd to have given me longer life,
And able means, we had not parted thus.
These are the whole contents:—and, good my lord,
By that you love the dearest in this world,
As you wish Christian peace to souls departed,
Stand these poor people's friend, and urge the king
To do me this last right.

Capucius. By heaven, I will,
Or let me lose the fashion of a man!

Katherine. I thank you, honest lord. Remember me
In all humility unto his highness:
Say his long trouble now is passing
Out of this world: tell him in death I bless'd him,
For so I will.—Mine eyes grow dim.—Farewell,
My lord.—Griffith, farewell.—Nay, Patience,
You must not leave me yet: I must to bed;
Call in more women.—When I am dead, good wench,
Let me be us'd with honour: strew me over

With maiden flowers, that all the world may know
I was a chaste wife to my grave. Embalm me,
Then lay me forth: although unqueen'd, yet like
A queen, and daughter to a king, inter me.
I can no more.— [*Exeunt, leading Katherine.*

CHRIST CHURCH, OXFORD.

PALACE AT GREENWICH. RETURNING FROM THE CHRISTENING.

ACT V.

SCENE I. *A Gallery in the Palace.*

Enter GARDINER, *Bishop of Winchester, a* Page *with a torch before him.*

Gardiner. It's one o'clock, boy, is't not?
Boy. It hath struck.
Gardiner. These should be hours for necessities,
Not for delights; times to repair our nature
With comforting repose, and not for us
To waste these times.—

Enter SIR THOMAS LOVELL.

Good hour of night, Sir Thomas!
Whither so late?

Lovell. Came you from the king, my lord?

Gardiner. I did, Sir Thomas; and left him at primero
With the Duke of Suffolk.

Lovell. I must to him too,
Before he go to bed. I'll take my leave.

Gardiner. Not yet, Sir Thomas Lovell. What's the matter?
It seems you are in haste: an if there be
No great offence belongs to't, give your friend
Some touch of your late business. Affairs that walk
(As they say spirits do) at midnight have
In them a wilder nature than the business
That seeks dispatch by day.

Lovell. My lord, I love you,
And durst commend a secret to your ear
Much weightier than this work. The queen's in labour,
They say, in great extremity; and fear'd
She'll with the labour end.

Gardiner. The fruit she goes with
I pray for heartily,—that it may find
Good time, and live; but for the stock, Sir Thomas,
I wish it grubb'd up now.

Lovell. Methinks I could
Cry the amen; and yet my conscience says
She's a good creature, and, sweet lady, does
Deserve our better wishes.

Gardiner. But, sir, sir,—
Hear me, Sir Thomas: you're a gentleman
Of mine own way; I know you wise, religious;
And, let me tell you, it will ne'er be well,
'Twill not, Sir Thomas Lovell, take't of me,

Till Cranmer, Cromwell, her two hands, and she,
Sleep in their graves.
Lovell. Now, sir, you speak of two
The most remark'd i' th' kingdom. As for Cromwell,
Beside that of the jewel-house, is made master
O' th' rolls, and the king's secretary; further, sir,
Stands in the gap and trade of more preferments,
With which the time will load him. Th' archbishop
Is the king's hand and tongue; and who dare speak
One syllable against him?
Gardiner. Yes, yes, Sir Thomas,
There are that dare; and I myself have ventur'd
To speak my mind of him: and, indeed, this day—
Sir, I may tell it you, I think—I have
Incens'd the lords o' th' council that he is—
For so I know he is, they know he is—
A most arch heretic, a pestilence
That does infect the land: with which they moved
Have broken with the king; who hath so far
Given ear to our complaint (of his great grace
And princely care, foreseeing those fell mischiefs
Our reasons laid before him), hath commanded,
To-morrow morning to the council-board
He be convented. He's a rank weed, Sir Thomas,
And we must root him out. From your affairs
I hinder you too long: good night, Sir Thomas.
Lovell. Many good nights, my lord. I rest your servant.
[*Exeunt Gardiner and Page.*

As LOVELL *is going out, enter the* KING *and the* DUKE OF SUFFOLK.

King Henry. Charles, I will play no more to-night:
My mind's not on't; you are too hard for me.
Suffolk. Sir, I did never win of you before.
King Henry. But little, Charles;

Nor shall not when my fancy's on my play.—
Now, Lovell, from the queen what is the news?
Lovell. I could not personally deliver to her
What you commanded me; but by her woman
I sent your message; who return'd her thanks
In the greatest humbleness, and desir'd your highness
Most heartily to pray for her.
King Henry. What say'st thou, ha?
To pray for her? what, is she crying out?
Lovell. So said her woman: and that her suff'rance made
Almost each pang a death.
King Henry. Alas, good lady!
Suffolk. God safely quit her of her burthen, and
With gentle travail, to the gladding of
Your highness with an heir!
King Henry. 'Tis midnight, Charles:
Prithee, to bed; and in thy prayers remember
Th' estate of my poor queen. Leave me alone,
For I must think of that which company
Would not be friendly to.
Suffolk. I wish your highness
A quiet night; and my good mistress will
Remember in my prayers.
King Henry. Charles, good night.—
[*Exit Suffolk.*

Enter SIR ANTHONY DENNY.

Well, sir, what follows?
Denny. Sir, I have brought my lord the archbishop,
As you commanded me.
King Henry. Ha! Canterbury?
Denny. Ay, my good lord.
King Henry. 'Tis true: where is he, Denny?
Denny. He attends your highness' pleasure.
King Henry. Bring him to us.
[*Exit Denny.*

Lovell [*Aside*]. This is about that which the bishop spake:
I am happily come hither.

Enter DENNY *with* CRANMER.

King Henry. Avoid the gallery.
[*Lovell seems to stay.*
Ha!—I have said.—Be gone.
What!— [*Exeunt Lovell and Denny.*
Cranmer. I am fearful.—Wherefore frowns he thus?
'Tis his aspect of terror: all's not well.
King Henry. How now, my lord! You do desire to know
Wherefore I sent for you.
Cranmer [*Kneeling*]. It is my duty
T' attend your highness' pleasure.
King Henry. Pray you, arise,
My good and gracious Lord of Canterbury.
Come, you and I must walk a turn together;
I have news to tell you. Come, come, give me your hand.
Ah, my good lord, I grieve at what I speak,
And am right sorry to repeat what follows.
I have, and most unwillingly, of late
Heard many grievous, I do say, my lord,—
Grievous complaints of you; which, being consider'd,
Have mov'd us and our council, that you shall
This morning come before us: where I know
You cannot with such freedom purge yourself,
But that, till further trial in those charges
Which will require your answer, you must take
Your patience to you, and be well contented
To make your house our Tower: you a brother of us,
It fits we thus proceed, or else no witness
Would come against you.
Cranmer [*Kneeling again*]. I humbly thank your highness,
And am right glad to catch this good occasion
Most throughly to be winnow'd, where my chaff

And corn shall fly asunder; for, I know,
There's none stands under more calumnious tongues
Than I myself, poor man.

King Henry. Stand up, good Canterbury:
Thy truth and thy integrity is rooted
In us, thy friend. Give me thy hand, stand up:
Prithee, let's walk. Now, by my holy dame,
What manner of man are you? My lord, I look'd
You would have given me your petition, that
I should have ta'en some pains to bring together
Yourself and your accusers; and to have heard you,
Without indurance, further.

Cranmer. Most dread liege,
The ground I stand on is my truth and honesty:
If they shall fail, I, with mine enemies,
Will triumph o'er my person, which I weigh not,
Being of those virtues vacant. I fear nothing
What can be said against me.

King Henry. Know you not
How your state stands i' th' world, with the whole world?
Your enemies are many, and not small; their practices
Must bear the same proportion: and not ever
The justice and the truth o' th' question carries
The due o' th' verdict with it. At what ease
Might corrupt minds procure knaves as corrupt
To swear against you: such things have been done.
You are potently oppos'd, and with a malice
Of as great size. Ween you of better luck,
I mean in perjur'd witness, than your Master,
Whose minister you are, whiles here he liv'd
Upon this naughty earth? Go to, go to:
You take a precipice for no leap of danger,
And woo your own destruction.

Cranmer. God and your majesty
Protect mine innocence, or I fall into
The trap is laid for me!

King Henry. Be of good cheer;
They shall no more prevail than we give way to.
Keep comfort to you; and this morning see
You do appear before them. If they shall chance,
In charging you with matters, to commit you,
The best persuasions to the contrary
Fail not to use, and with what vehemency
Th' occasion shall instruct you: if entreaties
Will render you no remedy, this ring
Deliver them, and your appeal to us
There make before them.—Look, the good man weeps:
He's honest, on mine honour.—God's blest mother!
I swear he is true-hearted; and a soul
None better in my kingdom.—Get you gone,
And do as I have bid you.—[*Exit Cranmer.*] He has strangled
His language in his tears.

Enter an Old Lady.

Gentleman [*Within*]. Come back: what mean you?
Lady. I'll not come back; the tidings that I bring
Will make my boldness manners.—Now, good angels
Fly o'er thy royal head, and shade thy person
Under their blessed wings!
King Henry. Now, by thy looks
I guess thy message. Is the queen deliver'd?
Say ay; and of a boy.
Lady. Ay, ay, my liege;
And of a lovely boy: the God of heaven
Both now and ever bless her!—'tis a girl
Promises boys hereafter. Sir, your queen
Desires your visitation, and to be
Acquainted with this stranger: 'tis as like you
As cherry is to cherry.
King Henry. Lovell,—

Enter LOVELL.

Lovell. Sir.

King Henry. Give her an hundred marks. I'll to the queen. [*Exit King.*

Lady. An hundred marks! By this light I'll ha' more.
An ordinary groom is for such payment:
I will have more, or scold it out of him.
Said I for this the girl was like to him?
I will have more, or else unsay't; and now,
While it is hot, I'll put it to the issue. [*Exeunt.*

SCENE II. *The Lobby before the Council-chamber.*

Enter CRANMER; Servants, Door-keeper, *etc., attending.*

Cranmer. I hope I am not too late; and yet the gentleman,
That was sent to me from the council, pray'd me
To make great haste. All fast? what means this? Ho!
Who waits there?—Sure, you know me?

Door-keeper. Yes, my lord;
But yet I cannot help you.

Cranmer. Why?

Door-keeper. Your grace must wait till you be call'd for.

Enter DOCTOR BUTTS.

Cranmer. So.

Butts [*Aside*]. This is a piece of malice. I am glad
I came this way so happily: the king
Shall understand it presently. [*Exit Butts.*

Cranmer [*Aside*]. 'Tis Butts,
The king's physician. As he pass'd along,
How earnestly he cast his eyes upon me!
Pray heaven he sound not my disgrace! For certain
This is of purpose laid by some that hate me
(God turn their hearts! I never sought their malice),

To quench mine honour: they would shame to make me
Wait else at door, a fellow counsellor
'Mong boys, grooms, and lackeys. But their pleasures
Must be fulfill'd, and I attend with patience.

Enter the King *and* BUTTS, *at a window above.*

Butts. I'll shew your grace the strangest sight—
King Henry. What's that, Butts?
Butts. I think your highness saw this many a day.
King Henry. Body o' me, where is it?
Butts. There, my lord:
The high promotion of his grace of Canterbury;
Who holds his state at door 'mongst pursuivants,
Pages, and footboys.
King Henry. Ha! 'Tis he indeed.
Is this the honour they do one another?
'Tis well there's one above 'em yet. I had thought
They had parted so much honesty among 'em
(At least, good manners) as not thus to suffer
A man of his place, and so near our favour,
To dance attendance on their lordships' pleasures,
And at the door, too, like a post with packets.
By holy Mary, Butts, there's knavery:
Let 'em alone, and draw the curtain close;
We shall hear more anon.— [*Exeunt.*

The Council-chamber.

Enter the Lord Chancellor, *the* DUKE OF SUFFOLK, EARL OF SURREY, Lord Chamberlain, GARDINER, *and* CROMWELL. *The Chancellor places himself at the upper end of the table on the left hand; a seat being left void above him, as for the Archbishop of Canterbury. The rest seat themselves in order on each side. Cromwell at the lower end, as secretary.*

Chancellor. Speak to the business, master secretary:
Why are we met in council?

Cromwell. Please your honours,
The chief cause concerns his grace of Canterbury.
Gardiner. Has he had knowledge of it?
Cromwell. Yes.
Norfolk. Who waits there?
Door-keeper. Without, my noble lords?
Gardiner. Yes.
Door-keeper. My lord archbishop;
And has done half an hour, to know your pleasures.
Chancellor. Let him come in.
Door-keeper. Your grace may enter now.
[*Cranmer approaches the council-table.*
Chancellor. My good lord archbishop, I'm very sorry
To sit here at this present and behold
That chair stand empty: but we all are men,
In our own natures frail, and capable .
Of our flesh; few are angels: out of which frailty
And want of wisdom you, that best should teach us,
Have misdemean'd yourself, and not a little,—
Toward the king first, then his laws, in filling
The whole realm, by your teaching and your chaplains
(For so we are inform'd), with new opinions,
Divers and dangerous; which are heresies,
And, not reform'd, may prove pernicious.
Gardiner. Which reformation must be sudden, too,
My noble lords; for those that tame wild horses
Pace 'em not in their hands to make 'em gentle,
But stop their mouths with stubborn bits, and spur them
Till they obey the manage. If we suffer,
Out of our easiness and childish pity
To one man's honour, this contagious sickness,
Farewell all physic: and what follows then?
Commotions, uproars, with a general taint
Of the whole state; as, of late days, our neighbours,
The upper Germany, can dearly witness,
Yet freshly pitied in our memories.

Cranmer. My good lords, hitherto, in all the progress
Both of my life and office, I have labour'd,
And with no little study, that my teaching
And the strong course of my authority
Might go one way, and safely; and the end
Was ever to do well: nor is there living
(I speak it with a single heart, my lords)
A man that more detests, more stirs against,
Both in his private conscience and his place,
Defacers of a public peace than I do.
Pray heaven the king may never find a heart
With less allegiance in it! Men that make
Envy and crooked malice nourishment
Dare bite the best. I do beseech your lordships,
That in this case of justice my accusers,
Be what they will, may stand forth face to face,
And freely urge against me.

Suffolk. Nay, my lord,
That cannot be: you are a counsellor,
And by that virtue no man dare accuse you.

Gardiner. My lord, because we have business of more moment,
We will be short with you. 'Tis his highness' pleasure,
And our consent, for better trial of you,
From hence you be committed to the Tower;
Where, being but a private man again,
You shall know many dare accuse you boldly,—
More than, I fear, you are provided for.

Cranmer. Ah, my good Lord of Winchester, I thank you;
You are always my good friend: if your will pass,
I shall both find your lordship judge and juror,
You are so merciful. I see your end;
'Tis my undoing. Love and meekness, lord,
Become a churchman better than ambition:
Win straying souls with modesty again,

Cast none away. That I shall clear myself,
Lay all the weight ye can upon my patience,
I make as little doubt as you do conscience
In doing daily wrongs. I could say more,
But reverence to your calling makes me modest.

Gardiner. My lord, my lord, you are a sectary;
That's the plain truth: your painted gloss discovers,
To men that understand you, words and weakness.

Cromwell. My Lord of Winchester, you are a little,
By your good favour, too sharp; men so noble,
However faulty, yet should find respect
For what they have been: 'tis a cruelty
To load a falling man.

Gardiner. Good master secretary,
I cry your honour mercy: you may, worst
Of all this table, say so.

Cromwell. Why, my lord?

Gardiner. Do not I know you for a favourer
Of this new sect? ye are not sound.

Cromwell. Not sound?

Gardiner. Not sound, I say.

Cromwell. Would you were half so honest!
Men's prayers, then, would seek you, not their fears.

Gardiner. I shall remember this bold language.

Cromwell. Do.
Remember your bold life too.

Chancellor. This is too much;
Forbear, for shame, my lords.

Gardiner. I have done.

Cromwell. And I.

Chancellor. Then thus for you, my lord.—It stands agreed,
I take it, by all voices, that forthwith
You be convey'd to th' Tower a prisoner;
There to remain till the king's further pleasure
Be known unto us. Are you all agreed, lords?

All. We are.
Cranmer. Is there no other way of mercy,
But I must needs to th' Tower, my lords?
Gardiner. What other
Would you expect? You are strangely troublesome.
Let some o' th' guard be ready there.

Enter Guard.

Cranmer. For me?
Must I go like a traitor thither?
Gardiner. Receive him,
And see him safe i' th' Tower.
Cranmer. Stay, good my lords;
I have a little yet to say.—Look there, my lords.
By virtue of that ring I take my cause
Out of the gripes of cruel men, and give it
To a most noble judge, the king my master.
Chamberlain. This is the king's ring.
Surrey. 'Tis no counterfeit
Suffolk. 'Tis the right ring, by heaven! I told ye all,
When we first put this dangerous stone a rolling,
'Twould fall upon ourselves.
Norfolk. Do you think, my lords,
The king will suffer but the little finger
Of this man to be vex'd?
Chancellor. 'Tis now too certain,
How much more is his life in value with him.
Would I were fairly out on't!
Cromwell. My mind gave me,
In seeking tales and informations
Against this man, whose honesty the devil
And his disciples only envy at,
Ye blew the fire that burns ye. Now have at ye.

Enter the King, *frowning on them; he takes his seat.*

Gardiner. Dread sovereign, how much are we bound to heaven
In daily thanks, that gave us such a prince;
Not only good and wise, but most religious:
One that in all obedience makes the church
The chief aim of his honour; and, to strengthen
That holy duty, out of dear respect,
His royal self in judgment comes to hear
The cause betwixt her and this great offender.

King Henry. You were ever good at sudden commendations,
Bishop of Winchester; but know, I come not
To hear such flattery now, and in my presence:
They are too thin and bare to hide offences.
To me you cannot reach you play the spaniel,
And think with wagging of your tongue to win me;
But whatsoe'er thou tak'st me for, I'm sure
Thou hast a cruel nature, and a bloody.—
Good man [*to Cranmer*], sit down. Now, let me see the proudest,
He that dares most, but wag his finger at thee:
By all that's holy, he had better starve
Than but once think this place becomes thee not.

Surrey. May it please your grace,—

King Henry. No, sir, it does not please me.
I had thought I had had men of some understanding
And wisdom of my council; but I find none.
Was it discretion, lords, to let this man,
This good man (few of you deserve that title),
This honest man, wait like a lousy footboy
At chamber door? and one as great as you are?
Why, what a shame was this! Did my commission
Bid ye so far forget yourselves? I gave ye

Power as he was a counsellor to try him,
Not as a groom. There's some of ye, I see,
More out of malice than integrity,
Would try him to the utmost, had ye mean;
Which ye shall never have while I live.

Chancellor. Thus far,
My most dread sovereign, may it like your grace
To let my tongue excuse all. What was purpos'd
Concerning his imprisonment was rather
(If there be faith in men) meant for his trial,
And fair purgation to the world, than malice,—
I'm sure, in me.

King Henry. Well, well, my lords, respect him:
Take him, and use him well; he's worthy of it.
I will say thus much for him: if a prince
May be beholding to a subject, I
Am, for his love and service, so to him.
Make me no more ado, but all embrace him:
Be friends, for shame, my lords!—My Lord of Canterbury,
I have a suit which you must not deny me;
That is, a fair young maid that yet wants baptism,
You must be godfather, and answer for her.

Cranmer. The greatest monarch now alive may glory
In such an honour; how may I deserve it,
That am a poor and humble subject to you?

King Henry. Come, come, my lord, you'd spare your spoons. You shall have
Two noble partners with you; the old Duchess of Norfolk,
And Lady Marquess Dorset: will these please you?
Once more, my Lord of Winchester, I charge you,
Embrace and love this man.

Gardiner. With a true heart
And brother-love, I do it.

Cranmer. And let heaven
Witness how dear I hold this confirmation.

King Henry. Good man! those joyful tears show thy true heart.
The common voice, I see, is verified
Of thee, which says thus, "Do my Lord of Canterbury
A shrewd turn, and he is your friend for ever."—
Come, lords, we trifle time away; I long
To have this young one made a Christian.
As I have made ye one, lords, one remain;
So I grow stronger, you more honour gain. [*Exeunt.*

SCENE III. *The Palace Yard.*

Noise and tumult within. Enter Porter *and his* Man.

Porter. You'll leave your noise anon, ye rascals: do you take the court for Parish-garden? ye rude slaves, leave your gaping.

[*One within.*] Good master porter, I belong to th' larder.

Porter. Belong to th' gallows, and be hang'd, you rogue! Is this a place to roar in?—Fetch me a dozen crab-tree staves, and strong ones: these are but switches to 'em.—I'll scratch your heads: you must be seeing christenings! Do you look for ale and cakes here, you rude rascals?

Man. Pray, sir, be patient: 'tis as much impossible,
Unless we sweep 'em from the door with cannons,
To scatter 'em, as 'tis to make 'em sleep
On May-day morning; which will never be.
We may as well push against Paul's as stir 'em.

Porter. How got they in, and be hang'd?

Man. Alas, I know not: how gets the tide in?
As much as one sound cudgel of four foot
(You see the poor remainder) could distribute,
I made no spare, sir.

Porter. You did nothing, sir.

Man. I am not Samson, nor Sir Guy, nor Colbrand,
To mow 'em down before me; but if I spar'd any,

That had a head to hit, either young or old,
Let me ne'er hope to see a chine again;
And that I would not for a cow,—God save her!

[*One within.*] Do you hear, master porter?

Porter. I shall be with you presently, good master puppy.—Keep the door close, sirrah.

Man. What would you have me do?

Porter. What should you do but knock 'em down by th' dozens? Is this Moorfields to muster in?

Man. There is a fellow somewhat near the door; he should be a brazier by his face, for, o' my conscience, twenty of the dog-days now reign in's nose: all that stand about him are under the line; they need no other penance. That fire-drake did I hit three times on the head, and three times was his nose discharged against me: he stands there, like a mortar-piece, to blow us. There was a haberdasher's wife of small wit near him, that rail'd upon me till her pink'd porringer fell off her head, for kindling such a combustion in the state. I miss'd the meteor once, and hit that woman, who cried out, "Clubs!" when I might see from far some forty truncheoners draw to her succour, which were the hope o' th' Strand, where she was quartered. They fell on; I made good my place; at length they came to th' broomstaff to me: I defied 'em still; when suddenly a file of boys behind em', loose shot, deliver'd such a shower of pebbles, that I was fain to draw mine honour in, and let 'em win the work. The devil was amongst 'em, I think, surely.

Porter. These are the youths that thunder at a playhouse, and fight for bitten apples; that no audience but the Tribulation of Tower-hill, or the limbs of Limehouse, their dear brothers, are able to endure. I have some of 'em in *Limbo Patrum*, and there they are like to dance these three days, besides the running banquet of two beadles that is to come.

Enter the Lord Chamberlain.

Chamberlain. Mercy o' me, what a multitude are here!
They grow still too; from all parts they are coming,
As if we kept a fair here! Where are these porters,
These lazy knaves?—Ye've made a fine hand, fellows:
There's a trim rabble let in. Are all these
Your faithful friends o' th' suburbs? We shall have
Great store of room, no doubt, left for the ladies,
When they pass back from the christening.

Porter. An't please your honour,
We are but men; and what so many may do,
Not being torn a pieces, we have done:
An army cannot rule 'em.

Chamberlain. As I live,
If the king blame me for't, I'll lay ye all
By th' heels, and suddenly; and on your heads
Clap round fines for neglect. Ye're lazy knaves;
And here ye lie baiting of bombards, when
Ye should do service. Hark! the trumpets sound;
They're come already from the christening.
Go, break among the press, and find a way out
To let the troop pass fairly, or I'll find
A Marshalsea shall hold ye play these two months.

Porter. Make way there for the princess!

Man. You great fellow,
Stand close up, or I'll make your head ache.

Porter. You i' th' camblet, get up o' th' rail;
I'll pick you o'er the pales else. [*Exeunt.*

SCENE IV. *The Palace at Greenwich.*

Enter Trumpets, sounding; then two Aldermen, Lord Mayor, Garter, CRANMER, DUKE OF NORFOLK, *with his marshal's staff,* DUKE OF SUFFOLK, *two* Noblemen *bearing great standing bowls for the christening gifts; then, four* Noblemen *bear-*

ing a canopy, under which the DUCHESS OF NORFOLK, *god-mother, bearing the child richly habited in a mantle, etc., train borne by a lady; then follows the* MARCHIONESS OF DORSET, *the other godmother, and ladies. The Troop pass once about the stage, and Garter speaks.*

Garter. Heaven, from thy endless goodness, send prosperous life, long, and ever happy, to the high and mighty princess of England, Elizabeth!

Flourish. Enter King *and Train.*

Cranmer. And to your royal grace, and the good queen, [*Kneeling.*
My noble partners and myself thus pray:—
All comfort, joy, in this most gracious lady,
Heaven ever laid up to make parents happy,
May hourly fall upon ye!

King Henry. Thank you, good lord archbishop;
What is her name?

Cranmer. Elizabeth.

King Henry. Stand up, lord.— [*The King kisses the child.*
With this kiss take my blessing: God protect thee!
Into whose hand I give thy life.

Cranmer. Amen.

King Henry. My noble gossips, ye have been too prodigal.
I thank ye heartily: so shall this lady,
When she has so much English.

Cranmer. Let me speak, sir,
For heaven now bids me; and the words I utter
Let none think flattery, for they'll find 'em truth.
This royal infant—heaven still move about her!—
Though in her cradle, yet now promises
Upon this land a thousand thousand blessings,
Which time shall bring to ripeness. She shall be
(But few now living can behold that goodness)

A pattern to all princes living with her,
And all that shall succeed: Saba was never
More covetous of wisdom and fair virtue
Than this pure soul shall be: all princely graces,
That mould up such a mighty piece as this is,
With all the virtues that attend the good,
Shall still be doubled on her: truth shall nurse her,
Holy and heavenly thoughts still counsel her:
She shall be lov'd and fear'd: her own shall bless her;
Her foes shake like a field of beaten corn,
And hang their heads with sorrow: good grows with her
In her days every man shall eat in safety
Under his own vine what he plants, and sing
The merry songs of peace to all his neighbours.
God shall be truly known; and those about her
From her shall read the perfect ways of honour,
And by those claim their greatness, not by blood.
Nor shall this peace sleep with her: but as when
The bird of wonder dies, the maiden phœnix,
Her ashes new create another heir,
As great in admiration as herself,
So shall she leave her blessedness to one
(When heaven shall call her from this cloud of darkness)
Who from the sacred ashes of her honour
Shall star-like rise, as great in fame as she was,
And so stand fix'd. Peace, plenty, love, truth, terror,
That were the servants to this chosen infant,
Shall then be his, and like a vine grow to him:
Wherever the bright sun of heaven shall shine,
His honour and the greatness of his name
Shall be, and make new nations: he shall flourish,
And, like a mountain cedar, reach his branches
To all the plains about him. Our children's children
Shall see this, and bless heaven.

King Henry. Thou speakest wonders.

Cranmer. She shall be, to the happiness of England,
An aged princess; many days shall see her,
And yet no day without a deed to crown it.
Would I had known no more! but she must die;
She must, the saints must have her: yet a virgin,
A most unspotted lily shall she pass
To th' ground, and all the world shall mourn her.

King Henry. O, lord archbishop!
Thou hast made me now a man: never, before
This happy child, did I get any thing.
This oracle of comfort has so pleased me,
That when I am in heaven I shall desire
To see what this child does, and praise my Maker.—
I thank ye all.—To you, my good lord mayor,
And your good brethren, I am much beholding:
I have receiv'd much honour by your presence,
And ye shall find me thankful.—Lead the way, lords:
Ye must all see the queen, and she must thank ye;
She will be sick else. This day, no man think
Has business at his house, for all shall stay:
This little one shall make it holiday. [*Exeunt.*

MEDAL OF JAMES I.

EPILOGUE.

'Tis ten to one, this play can never please
All that are here. Some come to take their ease,
And sleep an act or two; but those, we fear,
We've frighted with our trumpets; so, 'tis clear,
They'll say 'tis naught: others, to hear the city
Abus'd extremely, and to cry, "That's witty,"
Which we have not done neither: that, I fear,
All the expected good we're like to hear
For this play, at this time, is only in
The merciful construction of good women;
For such a one we show'd 'em. If they smile
And say 'twill do, I know within a while
All the best men are ours; for 'tis ill hap,
If they hold when their ladies bid 'em clap.

GOLD MEDAL OF HENRY VIII

NOTES.

ABBREVIATIONS USED IN THE NOTES.

Abbott (or Gr.), Abbott's *Shakespearian Grammar* (third edition).
A. S., Anglo-Saxon.
B. and F., Beaumont and Fletcher.
C., Craik's *English of Shakespeare* (Rolfe's edition).
Cf. (*confer*), compare.
Com., Milton's *Comus.*
D., Dyce.
F., Fowler's *English Language* (8vo edition).
F. Q., Spenser's *Faërie Queene.*
Foll., following.
Fr., French.
H., Hudson.
Id. (*idem*), the same.
Il Pens., Milton's *Il Penseroso.*
J. H., Rev. John Hunter's edition of *Henry VIII.* (London, 1865).
K., Knight.
Mer., Rolfe's edition of *The Merchant of Venice.*
N. F., Norman French.
P. L., Milton's *Paradise Lost.*
Prol., Prologue.
Rich., Richardson's Dictionary (London, 1838).
S., Shakespeare.
Shep. Cal., Spenser's *Shepherd's Calendar.*
Sr., Singer.
St., Staunton.
Temp. (followed by reference to *page*), Rolfe's edition of *The Tempest.*
V., Verplanck.
Var. ed., the *Variorum* edition of Shakespeare (1821).
W., White.
Wb., Webster's Dictionary (revised quarto edition of 1864).
Worc., Worcester's Dictionary (quarto edition).

The abbreviations of the names of Shakespeare's Plays will be readily understood; as *T. N.* for *Twelfth Night*, *Cor.* for *Coriolanus*, 3 *Hen. VI.* for *The Third Part of King Henry the Sixth*, etc. *P. P.* refers to *The Passionate Pilgrim*; *V. and A.* to *Venus and Adonis*; *L. C.* to *A Lover's Complaint*; and *Sonn.* to the *Sonnets.*

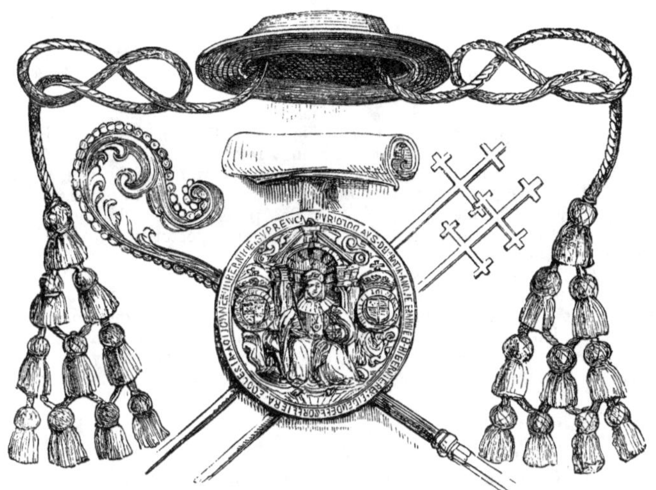

GREAT SEAL, CARDINAL'S HAT, ETC.

NOTES.

THE PROLOGUE.

DR. JOHNSON expressed the opinion that the Prologue and the Epilogue of this play were not written by Shakespeare, and the majority of the recent editors agree with him. Dyce says that, "whoever wrote them, they are manifestly not by Shakespeare." White remarks that there can hardly be a doubt on this point "in the mind of any reader who has truly appreciated the poet's style or his cast of thought." Knight, on the other hand, considers that "the prologue is a complete exposition of the *idea* of the drama," and that it is unquestionably Shakespeare's. See the quotation from Knight in the Introduction to this play (page 38). See also notes on the Epilogue of *The Tempest* (page 145).

If Shakespeare did not write the Prologue, it may be Ben Jonson's, as several of the critics have suggested.

Sad, high, and working. "Of a lofty character, and of stirring interest." St. reads "Sad and high-working."

May here find truth. On the repetition of the words *true* and *truth* in the prologue, and their possible connection with the original title of the play, see *Introduction*, page 10.

A fellow In a long motley coat. Alluding to the *fools* of the old plays and their professional costume. See *Mer.* p. 142 (note on *Patch*), and *Temp.* p. 131 (note on *Pied ninny*).

Guarded. Trimmed. See *Mer.* p. 140.

Opinion. Reputation. Cf. 1 *Hen. IV.* v. 2: "Thou hast redeem'd thy lost opinion." Or, as H. suggests, it may refer to the title *All is True*, "which would naturally beget an *opinion* or *expectation* of truth in what was to be shown; which opinion or expectation would be forfeited or destroyed by the course in question." The parenthetical addition, "We now intend only to make good that opinion or expectation," would then follow naturally enough.

Happiest hearers. As Steevens remarks, "*happy* appears to be used with one of its Roman meanings; that is, *propitious* or *favourable*" (cf. *Virgil*, Ecl. v.: "Sis bonus o felixque tüis"); "a sense of the word," he adds, "which must have been unknown to Shakespeare, but was familiar to Jonson." The poet's "small Latin," however, might easily have included this common meaning of a very common word.

ACT I.

SCENE I.—In the folio the play is divided into acts and scenes, and the stage directions are remarkably full, but there is no list of *dramatis personæ*.

Enter the Duke of Norfolk, etc. This Duke of Norfolk is Thomas Howard, son of the "Jockey of Norfolk" of *Richard III.* (v. 3), who was slain at Bosworth Field, and whose blood was attainted. His honours were, however, restored in his son, who became Lord Treasurer, Earl Marshal, and Knight of the Garter. This Duke of Buckingham is also the son and heir of the Duke in *Richard III.*, whose forfeited honours (see below, ii. 1) were restored in his son by Henry VII. He was Lord High Constable and a Knight of the Garter. Lord Abergavenny is George Neville, third baron of that name, and "one of the very few noblemen of his time who was neither beheaded himself, nor the son of a beheaded father, nor the father of a beheaded son. His brother, Sir Thomas, however, was compelled to follow the fashion" (W.).

Since last we saw. That is, saw each other. Cf. "When shall we see again?" in *T. and C.* iv. 4, and *Cymb.* i. 2. The third folio has "Since last we saw y' in France." Gr. 382.

Suns of glory. The third folio has "sons of glory," but the latter part of the line, and the recurrence of "these suns" below, are in favour of the original reading. Pope has borrowed the phrase in his Imitation of Horace's Epistle to Augustus: "Those suns of glory please not till they set."

The vale of Andren. In the second folio "Andren" is altered to "Arde," but S. gave the word as he found it in Holinshed's *Chronicle*: "The daie of the meeting was appointed to be on the thursdaie the seauenth of Iune, vpon which daie the two kings met in the vale of Andren."

Guynes and Arde. Two towns in Picardy, the one belonging to the English, the other to the French. The famous "Field of the Cloth of Gold" was in the valley between the two.

As they grew together. As *if*, etc. Gr. 107.

All the whole time. Cf. *M. of V.* iii. 4: "all my whole device;" 1 *Hen. VI.* i. 1: "all the whole army," etc.

Each following day, etc. "*Dies diem docet.* Every day learned something from the preceding, till the concluding day collected all the splendour of the former shows" (Johnson). On *it's*, see *Temp.* p. 120, or C. pp. 160–171.

Clinquant. W. says this is "a descriptive word, derived from the tinkle or gentle clash of metal ornaments," and this agrees with the definition in Rich.; but Worc. and Wb. both make it mean "glittering, shining," as do Nares, D. (*Glossary*), and the commentators generally. The word is evidently from the French *clinquant*, tinsel, glitter; but this, according to Wb. (see also Scheler, *Dict. d'Étymol. Franc.*), is from the Dutch *klinken*, to clink. The tinsel, named first from its *jingle*, naturally came to suggest rather its *glitter*. In B. and F. we find mention of "A clinquant petticoat of some rich stuff." S. uses the word only here.

Cherubins. On this form of the word (the only one found in the folio), see *Temp.* p. 115.

That their very labour. *So* that; as often. See Gr. 283.

As a painting. That is, it gave them rosy cheeks.

Him in eye, Still him in praise. Johnson quotes Dryden's "Two chiefs So match'd, as each seem'd worthiest when alone."

No discerner, etc. "No critical observer would venture to pronounce his judgment in favour of either king" (V.). On this use of *censure*, cf. *W. T.* ii. 1: "In my just censure, in my true opinion;" *Oth.* ii. 3: "mouths of wisest censure." The verb also means to pass judgment upon, to estimate, etc.; as in *K. John*, ii. 1: "whose equality By our best eyes cannot be censured." In *T. G. of V.* ii. 1, we have "Should censure thus *on* lovely gentlemen."

Bevis was believed. That is, the old romantic legend of Bevis of Southampton. This Bevis was a Saxon whom William the Conqueror made Earl of Southampton. His exploit of subduing the giant Ascapard is alluded to in 2 *Hen. VI.* ii. 3: "Peter, have at thee with a downright blow, as Bevis of Southampton fell upon Ascapart." Camden, in his *Britannia*, says that "while the monks endeavoured to extol Bevis by legendary tales, they have obscured and drowned his truly noble exploits."

As I belong to worship, etc. As I am of the more honoured class, and in that honour love and seek honesty, the cause of these triumphs and pleasures, however well related, must lose in the description part of that spirit and energy which were expressed in the real action (Johnson).

All was royal, etc. In the folio the reading is as follows:

> "*Buc.* All was Royall,
> To the disposing of it nought rebell'd,
> Order gaue each thing view. The Office did
> Distinctly his full Function: who did guide,
> I mean who set the Body, and the Limbes
> Of this great Sport together?
> *Nor.* As you guesse:
> One certes, that promises no Element
> In such a businesse.
> *Buc.* I pray you who, my Lord?"

Theobald arranged the passage as in the text, and has been followed by the more recent editors, with the exception of K. and V., who defend the original reading. K. says: "After the eloquent description by Norfolk of the various shows of the pageant, he makes a *general observation* that 'order' must have presided over these complicated arrangements—'gave each thing view.' He then asks, 'Who did guide?'—who made the body and limbs work together? Norfolk then answers, 'As you guess'—according to your guess, *one* did guide:—'one certes,' etc."

Certes. See *Temp.* p. 133.

No element. No "constituent quality of mind," as K. explains it; or, possibly, no "initiation, or rudimentary knowledge," as Johnson and D. interpret it.

Fierce vanities. *Fierce* here appears to mean "extreme, excessive." Cf. *T. of A.* iv. 2: "O the fierce wretchedness that glory brings!" Ben Jonson (*Poetaster*, v. 3) speaks of "fierce credulity."

Keech. A lump of fat. "It had a triple application to Wolsey, as a corpulent man, a reputed butcher's son, and a bloated favourite" (W.). In 1 *Hen. IV.* ii. 4, Prince Henry calls Falstaff a "greasy tallow-keech" ("Tallow Catch" in the folio).

Chalks successors their way. Cf. *Temp.* v. 1: "For it is you that have chalk'd forth the way."

Out of his self-drawing web, he gives us note. The folio reads,

"Out of his Selfe-drawing Web. O giues vs note," etc.

The correction is by Steevens, and is adopted by Capell (who suggests that the "O" is a misprint for *A* or *'a*, which is often used for *he*), D., and W. K. reads "—O! give us note!—" (that is, Mark what I say!), and is followed by V. and H. Both K. and H. speak of this as "the original reading," though it will be seen that it varies from the folio quite as much, to say the least, as the other emendation does. On *note.* see *Temp.* p. 126.

Heaven gives for him. Warburton (followed by D.) reads, "A gift that heaven gives; which brings for him," etc., and Johnson suggested "heaven gives to him;" but *for* may be explained by Gr. 149.

The file of all the gentry. The list of them. Cf. *Macb.* v. 2: "I have a file Of all the gentry."

To whom as great a charge . . . lay upon. Some editors read "Too, whom," etc. But double prepositions are not uncommon in S. See Gr. 407. H. suggests that the expression may be elliptical for "To whom *he gave* as great a charge, as he meant to lay upon *them* little honour."

His own letter . . . he papers. The folio reads,

—"his owne Letter
The Honourable Boord of Councell, out
Must fetch him in, he Papers."

Pope says: "He *papers*, a verb: his own letter, by his own single authority, and without the concurrence of the council, must fetch him in whom he papers down. I don't understand it, unless this be the meaning." This explanation is accepted by most of the editors, but some have read "the papers" (that is, "all communications on the subject," which he requires by "his own letter" to be addressed to himself), and St. conjectures "he paupers." We find *papers* as a verb in *Albion's England*, chap. 80:

> "Set is the soveraigne Sunne did shine when paper'd last our penns."

Have broke their backs with laying manors on them. Cf. *K. John*, ii. 1: "Bearing their birthrights proudly on their backs." Burton, in his *Anatomy of Melancholy* (ed. 1634), says: "'Tis an ordinary thing to put a thousand oakes, or an hundred oxen, into a sute of apparell, to weare a whole manor on his backe."

What did this vanity, etc. "What effect had this pompous show but the production of a wretched conclusion?" (Johnson.) Staunton says, "but furnish discourse on the poverty of its result."

Not values. See Gr. 305.

The hideous storm that follow'd. "Monday the xviii. of June was such an *hideous storme* of wind and weather, that many conjectured it did prognosticate trouble and hatred shortly after to follow between princes" (Holinshed).

Not consulting. That is, independently of each other.

Aboded. Foreboded. Cf. 3 *Hen. VI.* v. 6: "aboding luckless time." In the same play (iv. 7) we have the noun "abodements." "Budded," in Norfolk's reply, is probably a play upon "aboded."

The ambassador is silenc'd. "Refused an audience" (Johnson).

Marry, is't. On *marry*, see *Mer.* p. 138.

A proper title of a peace. A fine description of a *peace*, this making an ambassador hold his peace! On the ironical use of *proper*, cf. *Macb.* iii. 4:

> "O proper stuff!
> This is the very painting of your fear."

Our reverend cardinal carried. Managed. Cf. below (i. 2), "he'd carry it so, To make the sceptre his."

Like it your grace. May it like, or please, your grace. We have the full expression in v. 2: "Dread sovereign, may it like your grace," etc. Cf. *Hen. V.* iv. 1: "this lodging likes me better;" *Lear*, ii. 2: "his countenance likes me not," etc.

Where's his examination? That is, where is he to be examined?

So please you. *If* it please you. Gr. 133.

This butcher's cur. "Wolsey was not the son of a butcher, but, as we know by his father's will, of a substantial and even wealthy burgess of Ipswich, where, and in Stoke, he was a considerable landholder. A butcher might be all this now, and more, but not then" (W.).

Venom-mouth'd. The folio has "venom'd-mouth'd," which may be what S. wrote.

A beggar's book. A beggar's learning. "Although the duke is afterwards called 'a learned gentleman,' and is known from contemporary authority to have had a taste for letters, yet it is not out of character that he should here use the insolent and narrow tone of his order in those times" (V.). Collier's MS. corrector has "a beggar's brood," and Lettsom suggests "beggar's brat." Cf. 2 *Hen. VI.* iv. 7: "Because my book (that is, learning) preferr'd me to the king."

Temperance. Patience, moderation. Cf. *Cor.* iii. 3: "Being once chaf'd, he cannot Be rein'd again to temperance."

Bores me with some trick. "Undermines me with some device" (St.).

Anger is like a full-hot horse, etc. Cf. Massinger, *The Unnatural Combat:*

> "Let passion work, and, like a hot-rein'd horse,
> 'Twill quickly tire itself."

From a mouth of honour, etc. "I will crush this base-born fellow, by the due influence of my rank, or say that all distinction of persons is at an end" (Johnson).

Heat not a furnace, etc. Possibly, as Steevens suggests, an allusion to *Dan.* iii. 22.

Mounts the liquor. Cf. below (i. 2): "mounting his eyes;" and see *Temp.* p. 128.

More stronger. See *Mer.* p. 159 (note on *More elder*), and Gr. 11.

If with the sap of reason, etc. Cf. *Ham.* iii. 4:

> "Upon the heat and flame of thy distemper
> Sprinkle cool patience."

Whom from the flow of gall, etc. Whom I call so, not from mere bitterness of feeling, but from honest indignation.

Founts in July. The folio has "Founts in *Inly.*"

Equal ravenous. See Gr. 1.

Suggests the king. Incites or tempts the king. See *Temp.* p. 127, note on *Suggestion.*

Did break i' th' rinsing. The folio has "ith' wrenching," which is probably a corruption of "rinsing."

Count-cardinal. Wolsey is called "king-cardinal" in ii. 2. Pope reads here "court-cardinal," and has been followed by some editors.

Charles, the emperor. Charles V., emperor of Germany.

His colour. His pretext. Cf. *A. and C.* i. 3: "seek no colour for your going."

Visitation. Visit. See *Temp.* p. 130.

He privily. The "he" was added in the second folio.

Paid ere he promis'd, etc. "Gave a bribe before Wolsey gave a promise; and by Wolsey's acceptance of the bribe the suit was virtually granted before it was presented" (J. H.).

Foresaid. S. uses *foresaid* six times, *aforesaid* three times.

Something mistaken. Somewhat mistaken or misapprehended by *you.* On *something*, see *Mer.* p. 130, or Gr. 68.

He shall appear in proof. That is, *in which* he shall appear. For the ellipsis, see Gr. 394.

Device and practice. Intrigue and artifice. Cf. *Oth.* v. 2: "Fallen in the practice of a cursed slave;" *M. for M.* v. 1: "This needs must be practice," etc.

I am sorry To see you ta'en, etc. Johnson explains this, "I am sorry to be present and an eye-witness of your loss of liberty;" Staunton, "I am sorry, since it is to see you deprived of liberty, that I am a witness of this scene;" J. H. (incorrectly, I think), "called away from liberty to attend to such a business as this." Collier puts a colon after "liberty," and a comma after "present."

That dye is on me. The literal meaning of *attainder* is a *staining.*

Aberga'ny. The usual pronunciation of the name.

You shall to the Tower. See Gr. 405.

Attach Lord Montacute. Arrest him. Cf. *Oth.* i. 2: "I therefore apprehend and do attach thee." Lord Montacute was Henry Pole, grandson to George, Duke of Clarence, and eldest brother to Cardinal Pole. He was restored to favour at this time, but was afterwards arrested for another treason and executed.

Gilbert Peck, his chancellor. The folio has "his Councellour," but in ii. 1, "Sir *Gilbert Pecke*, his Chancellour," which agrees with Hall and Holinshed.

Nicholas Hopkins. The folio has "*Michaell Hopkins;*" probably, as W. suggests, from the printer's mistaking the abbreviation "*Nich.*" for "*Mich.*" K. retains the reading of the folio, thinking that "the poet might intend Buckingham to give the Nicholas Hopkins of the *Chronicles* a wrong Christian name in his precipitation." The Carthusians, or "monks of the Chartreuse," appeared in England about 1180, and in 1371 a monastery of the order was founded on the site of the present Charter-house (the name is a corruption of *Chartreuse*), in London.

Whose figure even this instant cloud, etc. "Whose" refers to "Buckingham," not to "shadow." "The speaker says that his life is cut short already, and that what they see is but the shadow of the real Buckingham whose figure is assumed by the instant [the present, the passing] cloud

DUKE OF BUCKINGHAM.

which darkens the sun of his prosperity. Johnson first proposed to read, 'this instant cloud puts *out*,' and in so doing diverted the minds of many readers (including editors and commentators) from the real meaning of the passage, and created an obscurity for them which otherwise might not have existed" (W.). Sr., V., and H. adopt Johnson's emendation.

SCENE II.—*I' th' level.* In the direct aim. See *Mer.* p. 131, note on *Level at;* and cf. *Sonn.* 117: "Bring me within the level of your frown, But shoot not at me."

Confederacy. Conspiracy.

Justify. Verify, prove. See *Temp.* p. 141, note on *Justify you traitors.*

The king riseth from his state. That is, from his throne. Cf. 1 *Hen. IV.* ii. 4: "This chair shall be my state, this dagger my sceptre," etc.

Of true condition. Of loyal character.

Putter-on. Instigator. Cf. *W. T.* ii. 1: "You are abus'd, and by some putter-on." "Put on" is often used with a like sense; as in *Ham.* iv. 7: "We'll put on those shall praise your excellence."

Such which breaks The sides of loyalty. On "such which," see Gr. 278. Collier's MS. corrector has "ties" for "sides."

Longing. Belonging. It is doubtful, however, whether the word is a *contraction* of "belonging," though Abbott (Gr. 460), W., and others print it "'longing." See Rich., under *long* and *belong;* and cf. *Mer.* p. 153 (note on *Bated*), and *Temp.* p. 118 (note on *Hests*). Examples of *long* with this sense are common in Old English; as in Chaucer, *Knightes Tale*, 1420: "That to the sacrifice longen schal." For examples in S., see *T. of S.* iv. 5; *All's Well*, iv. 2; *Cor.* v. 3; *Hen. V.* ii. 4, etc.

Spinsters. Spinners. See on this word Trench, *English, Past and Present*, Amer. ed. p. 121; also his *Select Glossary*, s. v.

Danger serves among 'em. Danger is often personified by our old poets; as by Chaucer, Gower, Skelton, and Spenser (*Var.* ed.).

Please you. If it please you. See *Mer.* pp. 134, 136.

I front but in that file, etc. Johnson says, "I am but first in the row of counsellors;" but Wolsey disclaims any priority. "I *face* in that file," he says, or "I am but *one* in the row." On *tell*, see *Temp.* p. 123.

But you frame, etc. But you originate these measures which are adopted by the council.

Too hard an exclamation. Too harsh an outcry against you. Cf. 2 *Hen. IV.* ii. 1: "this tempest of exclamation."

Bolden'd. Cf. *A. Y. L.* ii. 7: "Art thou thus bolden'd, man, by thy distress?" S. also used *embolden;* as in *M. W.* ii. 2, *T. of A.* iii. 5, etc. Abbott (Gr. 460) considers this a contraction of *emboldened.*

This tractable obedience, etc. Their resentment gets the better of their obedience. "This" is the folio reading, but Rowe (followed by D.) altered it to "That," and Collier's MS. corrector to "Their."

There is no primer business. No more urgent business. The folio has "no primer basenesse," which K. retains. D. calls it "the next thing to nonsense," and W. remarks that, though it has a meaning, "it is a meaning entirely inappropriate in the context." Warburton suggested "business," and Collier's MS. corrector has the same emendation.

To cope. To encounter. Cf. *A. Y. L.* ii. 1: "I love to cope him in these sullen fits;" *T. and C.* ii. 3: "Ajax shall cope the best." On another meaning of the word, see *Mer.* p. 160.

Sick interpreters. Ill disposed critics.

Once weak ones. Sometimes (at one time or another) weak ones. See C. p. 350, and cf. *Jer.* xiii. 27.

Not allow'd. Not approved.

Hitting a grosser quality. Suiting or gratifying a baser nature.

Stick them in our will. Bring them under arbitrary rule (after tearing them from the protection of the laws).

A trembling contribution. That is, that may well make us tremble. Collier's MS. corrector has "trebling." See Gr. 4 and 372.

Lop. The lop-wood, or smaller branches.

Hardly conceive. Have hard thoughts.

Is run in your displeasure. Has incurred (which is, literally, *run into*) your displeasure. See Gr. 295, and C. p. 304.

Complete. Accomplished. The accent is on the first syllable. Cf. *L. L. L.* i. 1: "A maid of grace and complete majesty;" *Ham.* i. 4: "That thou, dead corse, again in complete steel," etc. See Gr. 492. Below (iii. 2) we have the word with the ordinary accent: "She is a gallant creature and complete."

Feel too little. Experience, or suffer from them, too little.

First, it was usual for him, etc. Holinshed says: "And first he uttered that the duke was accustomed, by way of talk, to say how he meant so to use the matter that he would attain to the crown if King Henry chanced to die without issue; and that he had talk and conference of that matter on a time with George Nevill, Lord of Abergavenny, unto whom he had given his daughter in marriage; and also that he threatened to punish the cardinal for his manifold misdoings, being without cause his mortal enemy."

He'll carry it. See above (i. 1) on *Our reverend cardinal carried.* The folio has "hee'l" (not "hell," as W. says), which Rowe altered to "he'd." But, as D. remarks, "in such sentences we frequently find our early writers using *will* where we should use *would.*" Cf. *C. of E.* i. 2:

> "If I *should* pay your worship those again,
> Perchance you *will* not bear them patiently;"

and *Cor.* i. 9:

> "If I *should* tell thee o'er this thy day's work,
> *Thou'lt* not believe thy deeds."

Cf., a few lines above, "If we *shall* stand still, . . . We *should* take root;" and see Gr. 370, 371.

This dangerous conception, etc. "This particular part of this dangerous design" (Johnson). D. changes "This" to "His."

Not friended by his wish. See Gr. 145.

Deliver all. See *Temp.* p. 144, note on *I'll deliver all.*

Upon our fail. In case of our failing to have an heir.

Nicholas Henton. The folio reading, altered by some editors to "Nicholas Hopkins;" but the man was often called Henton, from the monastery to which he belonged. Holinshed says: "—being brought into a full hope that he should be king, by a vain prophecy which one Nicholas Hopkins, a monk of an house of the Chartreux order beside Bristow, called Henton, sometime his confessor, had opened to him."

His confessor. On the accent of *confessor*, see Gr. 492.

Under the confession's seal. The folio misprints "vnder the Commissions Seale," which was corrected by Theo. Holinshed says: "The duke in talk told the monk, that he had done very well to bind his chaplain, John de la Court, under the seal of confession, to keep secret such matter."

This whole passage is a close paraphrase of Holinshed: "The same duke, the tenth day of May, in the twelfth year of the King's reign, at London in a place called the Rose, within the parish of Saint Laurence Poultney, in Canwick street ward, demanded of the said Charles Knevet esquire what was the talk amongst the Londoners concerning the king's journey beyond the seas. And the said Charles told him that many stood in doubt of that journey, lest the Frenchmen meant some deceit towards the king. Whereto the duke answered, that it was to be feared, lest it would come to pass according to the words of a certain holy monk. For there is, saith he, a Chartreux monk that divers times hath sent to me, willing me to send unto him my chancellor. And I did send unto him John de la Court, my chaplain, unto whom he would not declare anything till de la Court had sworn to keep all things secret, and to tell no creature living what he should hear of him, except it were to me. And then the said monk told de la Court that neither the king nor his heirs should prosper, and that I should endeavour to purchase the good wills of the commonalty; for I the same duke and my blood should prosper, and have the rule of the realm of England."

With demure confidence, etc. "In a grave confidential manner this was then uttered with pausing intervals" (J. H.). On *demure*, cf. *A. and C.* iv. 9: "Hark! the drums Demurely (solemnly) wake the sleepers;" and Milton (*Il Pens.*): "Sober, steadfast, and demure."

To gain the love. The word "gain" was first added in the fourth folio.

'Twas dangerous For him. The folio has "For this," which was corrected by Rowe.

It forg'd him some design. It enabled him to contrive some plan (for obtaining the crown).

What! so rank? "What, was he advanced to this pitch?" (Johnson.)

Have put his knife into him. S. follows Hall and Holinshed closely here; and Hall followed the legal records. By an extract made by Vallant from the Year Book 13 Henry VIII., it appears that this monk said, "*et auxi que il disoit si le Roy avoit lui commis al' prison, donques il voul' lui occire ove son dagger.*" The record goes on, "*Mes touts ceux matters il denia in effect, mes fut trove coulp: Et pur ceo il avoit jugement comme traitre, et fuit decolle le Vendredy devant le Feste del Pentecost que fuit le* xiij *Jour de May avant dit. Dieu à sa ame grant mercy—car il fuit tres noble prince et prudent, et mirror de tout courtesie*" (W.).

Mounting his eyes. See above (i. 1) on *Mounts the liquor.*

His period. His end, the intended consummation of his treason. Cf. *M. W.* iii. 3: "the period of my ambition;" *Lear*, iv. 7: "My point and period will be throughly wrought." We find *period* as a verb in *T. of A.* i. 1: "Periods his comfort."

By day and night. An oath, not an expression of time. Cf. *Ham.* i. 5: "By day and night, but this is wondrous strange." Possibly we have another instance in *Lear*, i. 3: "By day and night, he wrongs me."

SCENE III.—*Enter the Lord Chamberlain*, etc. S. has placed this scene in 1521. Charles [Somerset], Earl of Worcester, was then Lord Chamberlain; but when the king in fact went in masquerade to Wolsey's house (1526), Lord Sands, who is here introduced as accompanying the chamberlain, held that office. This Lord Sands was Sir William Sands, created a peer in 1524, and made chamberlain on the death of the Earl of Worcester in 1526.

Mysteries. "Artificial fashions" (K.).

Never so ridiculous. Modern usage favours "ever so" rather than "never so," but F. (§ 523, n. 6) says that "either form is correct." See Gr. 52.

A fit or two o' th' face. A few grimaces.

Pepin or Clotharius. Clothaire and Pepin were kings of France in the sixth century. We find allusions to Pepin in *L. L. L.* iv. 1, and *A. W.* ii. 1, and to both him and Clothaire in *Hen. V.* i. 2.

Or springhalt. The folio has "A Spring-halt;" but, as V. suggests, S. was too well skilled in horseflesh to confound two diseases so different, not only in nature, but in external effect, as the spavin and the springhalt. There can be no doubt that "a" is a misprint for either "or" or "and."

And never see the Louvre. That is, although he has never been at the French court.

Fool and feather. The feathers in the hats of the French gallants and their English imitators are indirectly compared to those worn by the professional jester—the "feathers wagging in a fool's cap," as an old ballad has it.

Fireworks. There were displays of fireworks on the last evening of the interview on the Field of the Cloth of Gold; and hence the "travelled gallants," as Steevens suggests, "might have imbibed their fondness for the pyrotechnic art."

Tennis. From the fifteenth century the game of ball known as *tennis* had been a favourite amusement in France with all classes, from the monarch to the meanest of his subjects; and at this time it was coming to be no less popular in England.

Short blister'd breeches. "This word 'blister'd' describes with picturesque humour the appearance of the slashed breeches, covered as they were with little puffs of satin lining which thrust themselves out through the slashes" (W.).

Cum privilegio. With privilege; an allusion to the special rights and immunities conferred by *privilege*, in the legal sense.

'Tis time to give 'em physic. W. omits "time"—an obvious misprint.

Held current music. That is, find it held, or recognized, as good music. Some editors change "held to "hold."

Nor shall not. See *Mer.* p. 131 (note on *Nor refuse none*), and Gr. 406.

A going. See Gr. 24.

That said other. Who should say anything to the contrary. Cf. *Oth.* iv. 2: "If you think other;" and see Gr. 12.

He may. That is, may be generous.

Has wherewithal. He has the means. The ellipsis is a common one. See Gr. 400.

Sparing would show, etc. Parsimony would appear, etc.

So great ones. That is, so great examples.

My barge stays. That is, it is waiting to take us (from the palace at Bridewell) to York-place.

Your lordship shall along. Cf. *Ham.* iii. 4: "And he to England shall along with you." On this very common ellipsis, see Gr. 405.

YORK-PLACE.

SCENE IV.—*The Presence-chamber in York-place.* "Whitehall, or rather the Palace, for that name was unknown until after Wolsey's time, was originally built by Hubert de Burgh, the eminent but persecuted Justiciary of England during the reign of Henry III. He bequeathed it to the convent of Blackfriars in Holborn, and they sold it to Walter de Grey, Archbishop of York, in 1248. From that time it was called York House, and remained for nearly three centuries the residence of the prelates of that see. The last archiepiscopal owner was Wolsey, during whose residence it was characterized by a sumptuous magnificence that most probably has never been equalled in the house of any other English subject, or surpassed in the palaces of many of its kings." [Knight's *London*, i. 334.]

The details of this scene are from Cavendish,* who says: "And when it pleased the king's majesty, for his recreation, to repair unto the cardinal's house, as he did divers times in the year, at which time there wanted no preparation or goodly furniture, with viands of the finest sort that might be provided for money or friendship; such pleasures were then devised for the king's comfort and consolation as might be invented, or by man's wit imagined. The banquets were set forth, with masks and mummeries, in so gorgeous a sort and costly manner, that it was a heaven to behold. There wanted no dames or damsels meet or apt to dance with the maskers, or to garnish the place for the time, with other goodly disports. Then was there all kind of music and harmony set forth, with excellent voices both of men and children. I have seen the king suddenly come in thither in a mask, with a dozen of other maskers, all in garments like shepherds, made of fine cloth of gold, and fine crimson satin paned,† and caps of the same, with visors of good proportion of visnomy,‡ their hairs and beards either of fine gold wire or else of silver, and some being of black silk; having sixteen torch-bearers, besides their drums, and other persons attending upon them, with visors, and clothed all in satin of the same colours. And at his coming, and before he came into the hall, ye shall understand, that he came by water to the water gate, without any noise; where against his coming were laid charged many chambers, and at his landing they were all shot off, which made such a rumble in the air, that it was like thunder. It made all the noblemen, ladies, and gentlemen, to muse what it should mean coming so suddenly, they sitting quietly at a solemn banquet; under this sort: First, ye shall perceive, that the tables were set in the chamber of presence, banquet-wise covered, my lord cardinal sitting under the cloth of estate, and there having his service all alone; and then was there set a lady and a nobleman, or a gentleman and gentlewoman, throughout all the tables in the chamber on the one side, which were made and joined as it were but one table. All which order and device was done and devised by the Lord Sands, lord chamberlain to the king; and also by Sir Henry Guilford, comptroller to the king. Then immediately after this great shot of guns the cardinal desired the lord chamberlain and comptroller to look what this sudden shot should mean,

* We give the passage as quoted by Knight, in his *Pictorial Edition of Shakespeare*. The MS. copies of Cavendish vary a good deal in their readings.

† *Paned* means "ornamented with cuts or openings in the cloth, where other colours were inserted in silk, and drawn through" (Nares). Cf. Thynne's *Debate* (1580):

"This breech was paned in the fayrest wyse,
And with right satten very costly lyned."

‡ That is, physiognomy. Cf. *A. W.* iv. 5: "His phisnomy is more hotter in France," etc.

as though he knew nothing of the matter. They, thereupon looking out of the windows into Thames, returned again, and showed him that it seemed to them there should be some noblemen and strangers arrived at his bridge, as ambassadors from some foreign prince. With that quoth the cardinal, 'I shall desire you, because ye can speak French, to take the pains to go down into the hall to encounter and to receive them according to their estates, and to conduct them into this chamber, where they shall see us, and all these noble personages, sitting merrily at our banquet, desiring them to sit down with us, and to take part of our fare and pastime.' Then they went incontinent down into the hall, where they received them with twenty new torches, and conveyed them up into the chamber, with such a number of drums and fifes as I have seldom seen together at one time at any masque. At their arrival into the chamber, two and two together, they went directly before the cardinal where he sat, saluting him very reverently; to whom the lord chamberlain for them said: 'Sir, forasmuch as they be strangers, and can speak no English, they have desired me to declare unto your grace thus: They, having understanding of this your triumphant banquet, where was assembled such a number of excellent fair dames, could do no less, under the supportation of your good grace, but to repair hither to view as well their incomparable beauty, as for to accompany them at mumchance,* and then after to dance with them, and so to have of them acquaintance. And, sir, they furthermore require of your grace licence to accomplish the cause of their repair.' To whom the cardinal answered that he was very well contented they should do so. Then the maskers went first and saluted all the dames as they sat, and then returned to the most worthiest, and there opened a cup full of gold, with crowns and other pieces of coin, to whom they set divers pieces to be cast at. Thus in this manner perusing all the ladies and gentlewomen, and to some they lost, and of some they won. And thus done, they returned unto the cardinal, with great reverence, pouring down all the crowns in the cup, which was about two hundred crowns. 'At all!'† quoth the cardinal, and so cast the dice, and won them all at a cast, whereat was great joy made. Then quoth the cardinal to my lord chamberlain, 'I pray you,' quoth he, 'that you will show them, that it seemeth me that there should be among them some noble man whom I suppose to be much more worthy of honour to sit and occupy this room and place than I; to whom I would most gladly, if I knew him, surrender my place according to my duty.' Then spake my lord chamberlain unto them in French, declaring my lord cardinal's mind, and they rounding‡ him again in the ear, my lord chamberlain said to my lord cardinal: 'Sir, they confess,' quoth he, 'that among them there is such a noble personage, whom if your grace can appoint him from the other, he is contented to disclose himself, and to accept your place most worthily.' With that the cardinal, taking a good advisement among them, at the last quoth he:

* A game played either with cards or with dice; here the latter, as appears from what follows.

† That is, I throw for all the money. See Nares on "Have at all."

‡ To *round in the ear*, or simply *to round*, meant to whisper. See *K. John*, ii. 1: "rounded in the ear;" *W. T.* i. 2: "whispering, rounding," etc.

'Meseemeth the gentleman with the black beard should be even he.' And with that he arose out of his chair, and offered the same to the gentleman in the black beard, with his cap in his hand. The person to whom he offered then his chair was Sir Edward Neville, a comely knight, of a goodly personage, that much more resembled the king's person in that mask than any other. The king, hearing and perceiving the cardinal so deceived in his estimation and choice, could not forbear laughing; but plucked down his visor, and Master Neville's also, and dashed out with such a pleasant countenance and cheer, that all noble estates there assembled, seeing the king to be there amongst them, rejoiced very much. The cardinal eftsoons desired his highness to take the place of estate; to whom the king answered, that he would go first and shift his apparel; and so departed, and went straight into my lord's bedchamber, where was a great fire made and prepared for him, and there new-apparelled him with rich and princely garments. And, in the time of the king's absence, the dishes of the banquet were clean taken up, and the tables spread again with new and sweet perfumed cloths; every man sitting still until the king and his maskers came in among them again, every man being newly apparelled. Then the king took his seat under the cloth of estate, commanding no man to remove, but sit still, as they did before. Then in came a new banquet before the king's majesty, and to all the rest through the tables, wherein, I suppose, were served two hundred dishes or above, of wondrous costly meats and devices subtilly devised. Thus passed they forth the whole night with banqueting, dancing, and other triumphant devices, to the great comfort of the king, and pleasant regard of the nobility there assembled."

This noble bevy. The word *bevy* meant at first a flock of birds, especially quails; afterwards, a company of persons, especially ladies. Cf. Milton, *P. L.* xi. 582: "A bevy of fair women;" Spenser, *F. Q.* i. 9, 34: "A lovely bevy of faire Ladies sate." In *Ham.* v. 2, the folio has "the same Beauy," but the quartos, "the same breed." The word occurs nowhere else in S.

As first good company. The very best company. The folio points thus: "As first, good Company." Theo. printed "first-good," as K. does. Hanmer gave "As, first, good company, then good wine, good women." Halliwell conjectured "As far good;" D. has "As far as good," etc.; W., "first good;" V. and H., "first, good."

You're tardy. The folio has here, as in several places below, "y'are," which W. retains. See Gr. 461.

For my little cure. As regards my little charge. Gr. 149.

Such a bowl may hold. An ellipsis like that of *as* or *that* after *so;* as in *M. of V.* iii. 3: "So fond to come abroad." See Gr. 281, 282.

Beholding. See *Mer.* p. 135. W. gives the following from Butler's *Grammar* (1633), which had been imperfectly quoted by Boswell:

"*Beholding* to one:—of to *behold* or regard: which, by a *Synecdoche generis,* signifyeth to respect and behold, or look upon with love and thanks for a benefit received. . . . So that this English phrase, *I am beholding to you,* is as much as, I specially respect you for some special kindness: yet some, now-a-days, had rather write it *Beholden,* i. e., obliged, answering to that *teneri et firmiter obligari:* which conceipt would seeme the more probable, if to *beholde* did signifie to *holde*, as to *bedek* to *dek*, to *besprinkle* to *sprinkle*. But indeed, neither is *beholden* English, neither are *behold* and *hold* any more all one, than *become* and *come*, or *beseem* and *seem*."

If I make my play. "If I may choose my game" (Ritson).

Chambers discharged. See *Introduction*, p. 9.

I should judge now unhappily. Johnson explains *unhappily* as "unluckily, mischievously;" J. H. as "censoriously."

An't. See *Mer.* p. 131, or Gr. 101.

The Viscount Rochford. He was not made viscount until after the king had fallen in love with Anne. Cavendish says: "This gentlewoman was the daughter of Sir Thomas Bullen, Knight, being at that time but only a bachelor knight, the which afterwards, for the love of his daughter, was promoted to high dignities. He bare at diverse several times, for the most part, all the great rooms of the king's household, as comptroller, and treasurer, and the like. Then was he made Viscount Rochford; and at the last created Earl of Wiltshire, and knight of the noble order of the Garter, and, for his more increase of honour and gains, was made lord keeper of the privy seal, and one of the chiefest of the king's council."

I were unmannerly, etc. A kiss was the established reward of the lady's partner, which she could not deny, or he, without an open slight, refuse to take (W.).

Good my lord cardinal. On this transposition, see Gr. 13.

Knock it. A phrase "derived from beating time, or perhaps beating the drum" (V.). See Gr. 226.

ACT II.

The main points in the account of Buckingham's trial and his subsequent demeanour are taken from Hall. The duke admitted that he had listened to the prophecies of the Carthusian monk, but he eloquently and with "many sharp reasons" defended himself against the charge of treason. He was, however, convicted in the court of the lord high steward, by a jury of twenty-one peers, consisting of a duke, a marquis, seven earls, and twelve barons. The Duke of Norfolk, lord high steward on the occasion, shed tears as he pronounced the sentence; after which Buckingham, according to Hall, addressed the court as follows: "My lord of Norfolk, you have said as a traitor should be said unto, but I was never none. But, my lords, I nothing malign for that you have done to me; but the eternal God forgive you my death, and I do. I shall never sue to the king for life, howbeit he is a gracious prince, and more grace may come from him than I desire. I desire you, my lords, and all my fellows, to pray for me." The historian continues the narrative as follows:

"Then was the edge of the axe turned towards him, and so led into a barge. Sir Thomas Lovell desired him to sit on the cushions and carpet ordained for him. He said, 'Nay; for when I went to Westminster I was Duke of Buckingham; now I am but Edward Bohun, the most caitiff of the world.' Thus they landed at the Temple, where received him Sir Nicholas Vawse and Sir William Sandes, Baronets, and led him through the city, who desired ever the people to pray for him; of whom some wept and lamented, and said, 'This is the end of evil life; God forgive him! he was a proud prince! it is pity that he behaved him so against his king and liege lord, whom God preserve.' Thus about iiii of the clock he was brought as a cast man to the Tower."

Even to the hall. That is, to Westminster Hall.

WESTMINSTER HALL.

In a little. Briefly. Cf. "in a few" (*A. W.* i. 2), etc.

Was either pitied, etc. "Either produced no effect, or produced only ineffectual pity" (Malone).

He sweat extremely. Hall says: "The duke was brought to the bar sore chafing, and sweat marvellously."

Kildare's attainder. Hall says that in 1520 "the king, being informed that his realm of Ireland was out of order, discharged the Earl of Kildare of his office of deputy, and thereunto (by the means of the cardinal, as men thought) was appointed the Earl of Surrey, to whom the cardinal did not owe the best favour." Cf. what Surrey says (iii. 2): "You sent me deputy for Ireland," etc.

Whoever. For *whomsoever.* Cf. the frequent use of *who* for *whom* (see *Mer.* pp. 131, 143, and *Temp.* p. 113), etc.

Will find employment. That is, find employment *for.* Cf. *Mer.* p. 130 (note on *Would grant continuance*) and p. 153 (on *Send relief*).

Enter . . . . Sir William Sands. The folio has "*Sir Walter Sands,*" which is either a misprint or a slip of the pen.

Go home and lose me. That is, count me as lost to you.

Nor build their evils, etc. Steevens says: "*Evils,* in this place, are *foricæ.* So in *M. for M.* ii. 2:

—"'having waste ground enough,
Shall we desire to raze the sanctuary,
And pitch our evils there?'"

Henley (quoted by D.) remarks: "The desecration of edifices devoted to religion, by converting them to the most abject purposes of nature, was an Eastern method of expressing contempt. See 2 *Kings,* x. 27."

Make of your prayers. *Prayers* is here a dissyllable. See Gr. 480.

I as free forgive. On *free,* see Gr. 1.

No black envy shall mark my grave. The folio reads: "No blacke Enuy shall make my Graue." This is undoubtedly corrupt, for, as W. remarks, "although envy may, in a fine sense, be said to make a grave, it clearly cannot be the envy or the malice of the person for whom the grave is made." *Envy* often means hatred, or malice. See *Mer.* p. 151.

Till my soul forsake. The folio reading. Rowe added "me," which D. and Walker approve. K. remarks: "It is not difficult to see that S. had a different metaphysical notion from that of his editors: the *me* places the individuality in the body alone."

Sir Nicholas Vaux. Nicholas lord Vaux was son of Sir William Vaux, who fell at Tewkesbury, fighting on the side of Henry VI. The ballad, "The Aged Lover Renounceth Love," from which the verses sung by the grave-digger in *Hamlet* (v. 1) are a corrupt quotation, has usually been ascribed to Sir Nicholas, but is now known to have been written by his son, Thomas Vaux (J. H.).

Poor Edward Bohun. Buckingham's family name was Bagot; but one of his ancestors had married the heiress of the barony of Stafford, and their son assumed the name of Stafford, which was retained by his posterity. Buckingham, however, affected the surname *Bohun,* because he was descended from the Bohuns, Earls of Hereford, and held the office of lord high constable by inheritance of tenure from them.

I now seal it. That is, seal my truth, or loyalty, with blood.

And must needs say. On *needs*, see Gr. 25.

Be not loose. Be not incautious of speech, or "unreticent." Cf. *Oth.* iii. 3:

> "There are a kind of men so loose of soul,
> That in their sleeps will mutter their affairs."

The least rub. Cf. *K. John*, iii. 4: "each dust, each straw, each little rub;" *Cor.* iii. 1: "this so dishonour'd rub laid falsely I' the plain way of his merit."

From ye. On the use of *ye* and *you* in S., see Gr. 236.

Strong faith. "Great fidelity" (Johnson).

I am confident; You shall, sir. I have confidence in you; you shall have the secret.

Did you not of late days hear. We should say, Have you not lately heard, etc. See Gr. 347.

It held not. It did not hold good, did not prove true.

Allay those tongues. We should not now use "allay" in this connection; nor intransitively (=subside), as in *Lear*, i. 2: "with the mischief of your person it would scarcely allay."

And held for certain. And *it is* held, etc. See Gr. 382. Cf. above (i. 3): "Held current music too."

About him near. On the transposition, see Gr. 419 *a*.

To revenge him. On *him* for *himself*, etc., see Gr. 223.

Too open here. Too much exposed, in too public a place. Below (iii. 3) we have "in open"=in public.

SCENE II.—*Enter Suffolk.* This Duke of Suffolk was Charles Brandon, son of Sir William Brandon, who was Henry VII.'s standard-bearer at Bosworth Field, where he fell. The duke married Henry VIII.'s younger sister, the Queen Dowager of France, whose favoured lover he had been before her marriage to Louis XII. of France.

Well met, my lord chamberlain. Hanmer read "my good lord chamberlain," to mend the metre—a common impertinence with the early editors.

Turns what he list. Turns the wheel of fortune as he pleases.

These news are. S. uses *news* both as singular and plural. We find "these good news" and "this happy news" in a single scene (iv. 4) of 2 *Hen. IV.*

Have slept upon This bold bad man. That is, have been blind to his faults.

We had need pray. See Gr. 349.

Into what pitch he please. Of what stature, or height, he please. Cf. 1 *Hen. VI.* ii. 2:

> "I tell you, madam, were the whole frame here,
> It is of such a spacious lofty pitch,
> Your roof were not sufficient to contain 't."

For me, my lords. On *for*, see Gr. 149.

I not believe in. See *Temp.* p. 124 (note on *I not doubt*), or Gr. 305.

The king is discovered, sitting, etc. The stage direction in the folio, "conforming to the simple arrangements of our early stage" (W.), is, "*the King drawes the Curtaine and sits reading pensiuely.*"

Business of estate. S. uses *state* and *estate* interchangeably in their various senses. See *Mer.* p. 151.

Go to. See *Mer.* p. 136, and Gr. 185.

Enter Wolsey and Campeius. Lorenzo Campeggio (in its Latin form, *Campeius*) was a native of Bologna, and a man of great learning. He had been sent to England once before as legate, and was at that time made Bishop of Salisbury.

Have great care I be not found a talker. "I take the meaning to be, Let care be taken that my promise be performed, that my professions of welcome be not found empty talk" (Johnson). Steevens compares *Rich. III.* i. 3:

> —"we will not stand to prate;
> Talkers are no good doers."

So sick, though. "That is, so sick as he is proud" (Johnson).

I'll venture one have-at-him. I'll venture one thrust at him. The folio reads: "Ile venture one; haue at him." K. retains this, and says: "It appears to us that Norfolk means by 'I'll venture *one*'—I'll risk myself; and that Suffolk is ready to encounter the same danger—'I *another.*'" The second folio has "one heave at him." D., W., and H. read "one have-at-him" (or "one have at him"). Below (iii. 2) Surrey says to Wolsey, "Have at you;" and (v. 2) Cromwell to the council, "Now have at ye."

What envy reach you? What malice can reach you? See above (ii. 1) on *No black envy*, etc.

The Spaniard. That is, the Spanish court; hence the subsequent "they."

The clerks. The clergy.

Gave their free voices. The folio has "Haue their free voyces" (with a period after it), and this is retained by the editors generally. It can be explained only by assuming that "by a great freedom of construction the verb *sent* applies to this first member of the sentence, as well as to the second" (K.). "Proleptic omissions" do occur in S. (see Gr. 383, 394), but in this case I prefer to adopt W.'s emendation of "Gave." As he remarks, "that only the learned clerks should *have* their free voices is plainly absurd; although those who have not adopted Malone's violent misconstruction have been obliged to accept the absurdity. But we know that nearly all the learned clerks in Christian kingdoms *gave* 'their free voices' for Henry's divorce (the decisions of eight continental faculties of law and divinity to that effect are given in Hall's Chronicle); and therefore *Wolsey* may well say, 'Who can be angry now?'"

Such a man I would have wished for. See above (i. 4) on *Such a bowl may hold my thanks.*

Unpartial. Elsewhere (in four instances) S. has *impartial.* See *Mer.* p. 155, note on *Uncapable.* Cf. Gr. 442.

Two equal men. Two impartial men; referring to what has just been said.

A woman of less place. That is, of lower rank. On the omission of *which*, see Gr. 244.

Gardiner. Holinshed says: "The king received into favour Dr. Stephen Gardiner, whom he employed in services of great secrecy and weight, admitting him in the room of Doctor Pace, the which being continually abroad in ambassages (and the same oftentimes not much necessary) of the cardinal's appointment, at length took such grief therewith, that he fell out of his right wits." On his return, in 1527, from a mission to Rome respecting the divorce, Gardiner became secretary to the king, and in 1531 he was made Bishop of Winchester.

Kept him a foreign man still. Kept him constantly employed in foreign embassies. On *still*, see *Mer.* p. 128.

There's places. See *Temp.* p. 122, note on *There is no more such shapes.*

That good fellow. That is, Gardiner.

For such receipt of learning. For receipt of such learning; for the reception of such learned men. See Gr. 423, where many similar transpositions are cited.

SCENE III.—*The which to leave a thousand times*, etc. Theo. read "to leave is," and D. has "leave's;" but the ellipsis is a common one. See Gr. 403. On *the which*, see *Mer.* p. 133, and Gr. 270.

To give her the avaunt. To bid her begone—a *contemptuous* dismissal.

It is a pity, etc. A hardship that would move even a monster to pity. Gr. 244.

That quarrel, Fortune. According to Warburton, *quarrel* here means *arrow;* but, if it be what S. wrote, it is probably =*quarreler*, as Johnson explained it. Hanmer printed "quarr'ler." Collier's MS. corrector substitutes "cruel;" St. suggests "squirrel;" and Lettsom "that fortune's quarrel." D. favours Warburton's view; H. has "cruel;" W. "quarrel." *Quarrel* (=arrow) is used by Spenser, *F. Q.* ii. 11, 24: "But to the ground the idle quarrel fell." For other examples, see Nares.

'Tis a sufferance, etc. Cf. *A. and C.* iv. 2:

> "The soul and body rive not more at parting,
> Than greatness going off."

On *panging*, see Gr. 290.

A stranger now again. Reduced to the condition of a friendless stranger. Cf. *Lear*, i. 1: "Dower'd with our curse, and stranger'd with our oath."

Range with humble livers. Rank with those in lowly life.

Glistering. See *Mer.* p. 145, note on *Glisters.*

Our best having. Our best possession. Cf. *T. N.* iii. 5: "My having is not much."

Beshrew me. Curse me. See *Mer.* p. 143.

To say sooth. To tell the truth. See *Mer.* p. 127.

Maidenhead. Maidenhood. Cf. *Godhead*, etc. The suffixes *-hood* and *-head* are etymologically the same. See F. § 390, 5 (*e*), and Wb. under *Hood.*

Mincing. See *Mer.* p. 154.

Cheveril. Kid-skin. Cf. *R. and J.* iii. 1: "O, here's a wit of cheveril, that stretches from an inch narrow to an ell broad." In *T. N.* iii. 1, we find mention of "a cheveril glove."

A three-pence bow'd. An allusion to the old custom of ratifying an agreement by a bent coin; but there were no threepences so early as the reign of Henry VIII. (Fairholt.) *Hire* is here a dissyllable. Gr. 480.

To queen it. See Gr. 226 and 290.

Pluck off a little. Take off a little from the rank; that is, come down from a duke to a count.

An emballing. A coronation; referring to the *ball* placed in the left hand of the queen as one of the insignia of royalty.

For Carnarvonshire. That is, for a single Welsh county.

Long'd. See on this word above, i. 2.

High note's Ta'en. High note (or notice) is taken.

His good opinion, etc. The folio has "opinion of you, to you;" etc.

More than my all is nothing. "Not only my *all is nothing,* but if my all were more than it is, it were still nothing" (Johnson).

Beseech your lordship. See Gr. 401.

Fair conceit. Good opinion. See C. p. 202.

A gem To lighten all this isle. "Perhaps alluding to the carbuncle, a gem supposed to have intrinsic light, and to shine in the dark" (Johnson).

Come pat betwixt, etc. Hit the right moment between too early, etc.

Fie, fie upon, etc. The folio has "fye, fye, fye vpon," etc.

This compell'd fortune. This fortune thrust upon one. On the accent of *compell'd,* see Gr. 492.

Forty pence. This sum, being half a noble (or one sixth of a pound), was a common one for a wager. Steevens quotes sundry illustrations of this from old plays.

The mud in Egypt. The land fertilized by the overflow of the Nile.

More thousands. The folio has "mo" for "more," as often. See C. p. 213.

On't. See *Mer.* p. 143 (note on *Glad on't*), or Gr. 182.

If this salute my blood a jot. "Salute here means *move,* or *exhilarate*" (St.). Cf. *Sonn.* 121: "Give salutation to my sportive blood." W. quotes Daniel's *Civil Wars,* bk. ii.:

> "He that in glorie of his Fortune sate,
> Admiring what he thought could never be,
> Did feele his bloud within salute his state," etc.

Collier's MS. corrector alters "salute" to "elate."

It faints me. It makes my heart faint. See Gr. 297.

Do not deliver. See above (i. 2) on *Deliver all with charity.*

SCENE IV.—This long stage direction is from the folio, and conforms to the description of the trial in Holinshed and Cavendish.

Sennet. This word (also written *sennit, senet, synnet, cynet, signet,* and *signate*) occurs often in the stage directions of old plays, and, as Nares remarks, "seems to indicate a particular set of notes on the trumpet, or cornet, different from a flourish." In Dekker's *Satiromastix* (1602) we find, "Trumpets sound a flourish, and then a sennet." The etymology of the word is doubtful.

Pillars belonged to the insignia of cardinals. In the Life of Sir Thomas More we find mention of "his maces and pillars" in connection with Wolsey. The *silver crosses,* according to Holinshed, were emblems, "the one of his archbishopric and the other of his legacy, borne before him whithersoever he went or rode, by two of the tallest priests that he could get within the realm." Steevens quotes a satire on Wolsey, by William Roy, published at some time between the execution of Buckingham and the repudiation of Katherine:

"With worldly pompe incredible,
Before him rydeth two prestes stronge;
And they bear two crosses right longe,
Gapynge in every man's face:
After them folowe two laye men secular,
And each of theym holdyn a pillar,
In their hondes steade of a mace."

The queen . . . goes about the court. Cavendish says: "Then he called also the queen, by the name of 'Katherine queen of England, come into the court;' who made no answer to the same, but rose up incontinent out of her chair, where as she sat; and because she could not come directly to the king for the distance which severed them, she took pain to go about unto the king, kneeling down at his feet," etc.

I desire you do . . . and to bestow. See *Temp.* p. 131 (note on *Than to suffer*), or Gr. 350.

This speech of the queen follows Cavendish closely, as a brief extract from his account of the trial will show: "Sir," quoth she, "I beseech you for all the loves that hath been between us, and for the love of God, let me have justice and right; take of me some pity and compassion, for I am a poor woman and a stranger born out of your dominion; I have here no assured friend, and much less indifferent counsel; I flee to you as to the head of justice within this realm. Alas! sir, wherein have I offended you, or what occasion of displeasure have I designed against your will and pleasure; intending, as I perceive, to put me from you? I take God and all the world to witness that I have been to you a true, humble, and obedient wife, ever conformable to your will and pleasure, that never said or did anything to the contrary thereof, being always well pleased and contented with all things wherein you had any delight or dalliance, whether it were in little or much; I never grudged in word or countenance, or showed a visage or spark of discontentation. I loved all those whom ye loved only for your sake, whether I had cause or no, and whether they were my friends or my enemies."

No judge indifferent. No impartial judge. Cf. *Rich. II.* ii. 3: "Look at my wrongs with an indifferent eye." See also the quotation from Cavendish in the preceding note.

Have I not strove. See *Mer.* p. 141 (note on *Not undertook*), and Gr. 343.

He were mine enemy. See Gr. 301 and 237.

That had to him deriv'd your anger. That had brought upon himself your anger. Cf. *A. W.* v. 3: "Things which would derive me ill will to speak of."

Nay, gave notice. Nay, *I* gave notice. Gr. 401. Hanmer and Johnson read "gave not notice." The folio has an interrogation mark after "discharg'd."

Against your sacred person. That is, *aught* against it.

Reputed for a prince. See Gr. 148.

One The wisest. Cf. below, in this scene, "spoke one the least word;" and see Gr. 18.

And of your choice. Holinshed says that Katherine "elected to be of her counsel" the Archbishop of Canterbury, the bishops of Ely, Rochester, and St. Asaph, and others.

That longer you desire the court. That you desire the court to delay proceedings. The fourth folio has "defer the court," which D. adopts.

It is you Have blown. See Gr. 244.

I utterly abhor, etc. Blackstone remarks that *abhor* and *refuse* are technical terms of the canon law, corresponding to the Latin *detestor* and *recuso;* but, as W. suggests, it is doubtful whether S. meant to use them technically. Holinshed says that the queen "openly protested that she did utterly abhor, refuse, and forsake such a judge."

Have stood to charity. Cf. *Ham.* iv. 5: "To this point I stand." Gr. 187.

The consistory. The college of cardinals.

As you have done my truth. If he know. The folio reading. Hanmer (followed by D. and H.) read "But if he know."

The which . . . speak in. See Gr. 270 and 424.

You sign your place, etc. "By your outward meekness and humility, you *show* that you are of an holy order, but, etc." (Johnson.)

Where powers are your retainers, etc. "What an image is presented of an unscrupulous but most able man, to say that his *powers* are used as the mere agents of his pleasures, and his *words*, without regard to the general obligation of truth, are 'domestics' who serve but his will" (K.).

You tender more. You value or regard more. See *Temp.* p. 127.

'Fore his Holiness. On *'fore*, see Gr. 460.

She curtsies to the King, and offers to depart. Cavendish says: "And with that she rose up, making a low curtsy to the king, and so departed from thence. Many supposed that she would have resorted again to her former place, but she took her way straight out of the house, leaning, as she was wont to do, upon the arm of her general receiver, called Master Griffith. And the king, being advertised of her departure, commanded the crier to call her again, who called her by the name of 'Katherine queen of England, come into the court.' With that quoth Master Griffith, 'Madam, ye be called again.' 'On, on,' quoth she, 'it maketh no matter, for it is no indifferent court for me, therefore I will not tarry. Go on your ways.' And thus she departed out of that court, without any farther answer at that time, or at any other, nor would never appear at any other court after."

That man . . . let him. See Gr. 414.

Fully satisfied. Fully indemnified for the injury done him.

The passages made toward it. The approaches made toward it. Steevens explained "made" as "*closed* or *fastened*," putting a colon after "hindered."

My conscience first received. Cavendish makes the king say, "It was a certain scrupulosity that pricked my conscience upon divers words that were spoken at a certain time by the Bishop of Bayonne," etc. It was, in fact, the Bishop of Tarbes. See Froude *History of England*, vol. i. p. 114 (Amer. ed.).

The debating A marriage. On *the*, see Gr. 93. The folio misprints "And Marriage."

In the progress of this business, etc. "And upon the resolution and determination thereof, he desired respite to advertise the king his master thereof, whether our daughter Mary should be legitimate in respect of the marriage which was sometime between the queen here and my brother the late Prince Arthur. These words were so conceived within my scrupulous conscience, that it bred a doubt within my breast, which doubt pricked, vexed, and troubled so my mind, and so disquieted me, that I was in great doubt of God's indignation" (Cavendish).

Advertise. Accented on the penult. See Gr. 491.

Sometimes. Formerly. See *Mer.* p. 130.

The bosom of my conscience, etc. According to Holinshed, the king said, "Which words, once conceived within the secret bottom of my conscience," etc. Theo. therefore altered "bosom" to "bottom," which D. also adopts. In the next line the folio has "a spitting power;" a misprint corrected in the second folio.

Thus hulling in, etc. Cavendish's words are, "Thus being troubled in waves of a scrupulous conscience;" and Holinshed's, "Thus my conscience being tossed in the waves of a scrupulous mind." To *hull*, as explained by Steevens, is to drift about *dismasted;* but according to Rich. (see also Wb.), "a ship is said to hull when all her sails are taken down, and she floats to and fro." This is obviously the meaning in *Rich. III.* iv. 3:

> "And there they hull, expecting but the aid
> Of Buckingham to welcome them ashore."

Cf. Milton, *P. L.* xi. 840: "He look'd, and saw the ark hull on the flood."

And yet not well. That is, and not yet well. See *Mer.* p. 146 (note on *Yet have I not*), or Gr. 76.

First, I began in private, etc. "I moved it in confession to you, my lord of Lincoln, then my ghostly father. And forasmuch as then you yourself were in some doubt, you moved me to ask the counsel of all these my lords. Whereupon I moved you, my lord of Canterbury, first to have your licence, inasmuch as you were metropolitan, to put this matter in question; and so I did of all of you, my lords" (Holinshed).

So please your highness. See Gr. 133.

That I committed, etc. "That I committed to doubt, repressed under hesitation, the most forward opinion of my own mind" (J. H.).

Drives this forward. The folio reading, altered to "Drive" by the editors generally. But see *Mer.* p. 136 (note on *Dealings teaches them suspect*), *Temp.* p. 110 (note on *What cares these roarers*), and Gr. 333.

Paragon'd. Extolled as a paragon. See Gr. 290.

Meanwhile must be, etc. See Gr. 404.

I may perceive. See *Mer.* p. 133 (note on *May you stead me?*), or Gr. 307, 309.

Prithee, return. Cranmer was at this time abroad on an embassy connected with this business of the divorce. See below (iii. 2) where Suffolk tells Norfolk that Cranmer "is return'd in his opinions," etc. Some of the earlier editors, not understanding this, added here the marginal direction, "[*The King speaks to Cranmer.*"

Set on. We use this phrase only in the sense of incite, or instigate (as in *T. N.* v. 1: "I was set on to do't"); but in S. it also means to begin, proceed, lead the way, set out, etc. Cf. *J. C.* i. 2: "Set on: and leave no ceremony out;" *M. for M.* iii. 1: "To-morrow you set on;" 1 *Hen. IV.* v. 2: "Now—Esperance! Percy!—and set on," etc.

CARDINAL WOLSEY.

ACT III.

SCENE I.—The visit of Wolsey and Campeius to Katherine is thus described by Cavendish:*

"And then my lord rose up and made him ready, taking his barge, and went straight to Bath Place to the other cardinal, and so went together unto Bridewell, directly to the queen's lodging; and they, being in her chamber of presence, showed to the gentleman usher that they came to speak with the queen's grace. The gentleman usher advertised the queen thereof incontinent. With that she came out of her privy chamber with a skein of white thread about her neck, into the chamber of presence, where the cardinals were giving of attendance upon her coming. At

* As quoted by Knight.

whose coming quoth she, 'Alack, my lords, I am very sorry to cause you to attend upon me; what is your pleasure with me?' 'If it please you,' quoth my lord cardinal, 'to go into your privy chamber, we will show you the cause of our coming.' 'My lord,' quoth she, 'if you have anything to say, speak it openly before all these folks, for I fear nothing that ye can say or allege against me, but that I would all the world should both hear and see it; therefore I pray you speak your minds openly.' Then began my lord to speak to her in Latin. 'Nay, good my lord,' quoth she, 'speak to me in English I beseech you; although I understand Latin.' 'Forsooth then,' quoth my lord, 'Madam, if it please your grace, we came both to know your mind, how ye be disposed to do in this matter between the king and you, and also to declare secretly our opinions and our counsel unto you, which we have intended of very zeal and obedience that we bear to your grace.' 'My lords, I thank you then,' quoth she, 'of your good wills; but to make answer to your request I cannot so suddenly, for I was set among my maidens at work, thinking full little of any such matter, wherein there needeth a large deliberation, and a better head than mine, to make answer to so noble wise men as ye be; I had need of good counsel in this case, which toucheth me so near; and for any counsel or friendship that I can find in England, they are nothing to my purpose or profit. Think you, I pray you, my lords, will any Englishman counsel or be friendly unto me against the king's pleasure, they being his subjects? Nay, forsooth, my lords! and for my counsel in whom I do intend to put my trust be not here; they be in Spain, in my native country. Alas, my lords! I am a poor woman lacking both wit and understanding sufficiently to answer such approved wise men as ye be both, in so weighty a matter. I pray you to extend your good and indifferent minds in your authority unto me, for I am a simple woman, destitute and barren of friendship and counsel here in a foreign region; and as for your counsel, I will not refuse, but be glad to hear.'

"And with that she took my lord by the hand, and led him into her privy chamber, with the other cardinal, where they were in long communication: we, in the other chamber, might sometime hear the queen speak very loud, but what it was we could not understand. The communication ended, the cardinals departed, and went directly to the king, making to him relation of their talk with the queen, and after resorted home to their houses to supper."

Wench. See *Temp.* p. 115.

Orpheus. See *Mer.* p. 163.

There had made a lasting spring. Thus in the folio; but misprinted "There had been," etc., in many editions.

Killing care. That killing care, etc. The ellipsis sometimes occurs after *such*, as after *so* (Gr. 282). K. puts a colon after "art;" but the folio has a comma.

Wait in the presence. That is, in the presence chamber.

They should be good men, etc. "Being churchmen they should be virtuous, and every business they undertake as righteous as their sacred office, but all hoods, etc." (Malone.) *Cucullus non facit monachum* is an old Latin proverb.

Part of a housewife, etc. To some extent a housewife; I would fain be wholly one, that I may be prepared for the worst that may happen.

O' my conscience. On *of* in adjurations, see Gr. 169.

Envy and base opinion set against 'em. Malice and calumny pitted against them. See above (ii. 1) on *No black envy.*

So even. So consistent.

If your business, etc. If your business is with me, and concerning my conduct as a wife. Mason read "wise" for "wife," explaining the passage thus: "If your business relates to me, or to anything of which I have any knowledge." D. adopts this emendation, which W. also regards with favour; but it seems to me quite as awkward as the original reading.

Tanta est, etc. "So great is our integrity of purpose towards thee, most serene princess."

More strange, suspicious. Perhaps we ought to read "more strange-suspicious," as Abbott suggests (Gr. 2).

And service to his majesty and you. Edwards suggested that this line and the next had been accidentally transposed; but, as W. remarks, "integrity cannot alone breed suspicion; it must be joined with misunderstood service to produce such an effect."

And comforts to your cause. The folio has "our cause," which was corrected in the second folio.

Which was too far. Cf. i. 1: "O you go far."

My weak wit. My weak judgment, or understanding. Cf. *J. C.* iii. 2: "For I have neither wit, nor words, nor worth." The word is also used by S. in its modern sense; as in *Much Ado*, i. 1: "they never meet but there is a skirmish of wit between them." See C. p. 316.

For her sake that I have been. For the sake of the royalty that has been mine.

Though he be grown so desperate, etc. Though he be so rash as to express an honest opinion. Johnson paraphrases the passage thus: "Do you think that any Englishman dare advise me; or, if any man should venture to advise with honesty, that he could live?"

Weigh out. I think this means to estimate fairly, to consider impartially. Johnson hesitated between "deliberate upon, consider with due attention," and "counterbalance, counteract with equal force."—*Afflictions* is a quadrisyllable; like "distraction," a few lines below.

Much Both for your honour better. Much better, etc. Gr. 419 *a*, 420.

You'll part away. On *part*=depart, see *Mer.* p. 145.

The more shame for ye. "If I mistake you, it is by your fault, not mine; for I thought you good" (Johnson). On *ye*, see Gr. 236.

Churchmen's habits. Priestly vestments; "glistering semblances of piety" (*Hen. V.* ii. 2).

Superstitious to him. "That is, served him with superstitious attention; done more than was required" (Johnson).

A constant woman to her husband. A woman constant to her husband. See Gr. 419 *a*.

Ye have angels' faces, etc. Perhaps "an allusion to the saying attributed to St. Augustine, *Non Angli sed Angeli*" (D.).* Cf. Greene's *Spanish Mas-*

* According to Beda, the paternity of this pun belongs to Pope Gregory the Great,

querado: "England, a little island, where, as Saint Augustin saith, there be people with angel faces, so the inhabitants have the courage and hearts of lions."

Like the lily, etc. Cf. Spenser, *F. Q.* ii. 6, 16: "The lilly, Lady of the flowring field."

Grow as terrible as storms. Lord Essex was charged with saying, in a letter written in 1598 to the lord keeper, "There is no tempest to the passionate indignation of a prince" (Malone).

If I have us'd myself, etc. If I have deported myself.

SCENE II.—*Force them.* Enforce or urge them. Cf. *Cor.* iii. 2: "Why force you this?" *M. for M.* iii. 1: "bite the law by the nose, When he would force it."

If you omit The offer, etc. If you neglect this opportunity. See *Temp.* p. 125, note on *Omit the heavy offer of it.*

Have uncontemn'd, etc. "Have not gone by him contemned or neglected" (Johnson). As Mason remarks, the negative in "uncontemn'd" is extended to "neglected."

Gives way to us. Leaves a way open to us. Cf. *J. C.* ii. 3: "Security gives way to conspiracy."

He's settled, etc. "He is fixed in the king's displeasure, never to get out of it" (J. H.).

The cardinal's letter. The folio has "The Cardinals Letters;" but below we find "this Letter of the Cardinals" and "the Letter (as I liue) with all the Businesse I writ too's Holinesse."

Will this work? "Will this influence the king against him?" (J. H.)

How he coasts And hedges, etc. Creeps along by coast and hedge. As Mason remarks, "*hedging* is by land what *coasting* is by sea. On *he*, see Gr. 414.

Now all my joy, etc. The folio reading, followed by K., D., and W. Capell, Collier's MS. corrector, and H. read, "Now may all joy;" and some editors have "Now all joy." W. compares B. and F., *Coxcomb*, iv. 4: "Now all my blessing on thee!"—*Trace* is to follow; as in *Macb.* iv. 1: "all unfortunate souls That trace him in his line."

All men's. All men's *amen;* with perhaps a play upon *amen.*

But young, etc. But recent, and had better not be told to everybody.

A gallant creature, and complete. Cf. the accent of *complete* with that in "This man so complete," i. 2—the only other instance of the word in this play. Gr. 492.

I persuade me. See Gr. 223.

Memoriz'd. Made memorable. Cf. *Macb.* i. 2: "Or memorize another Golgotha."

Digest this letter. Cf. *L. L. L.* v. 2:

"For it can never be
They will digest this harsh indignity."

He is return'd in his opinions, etc. "The construction is here difficult,

who, on seeing some Saxon youths offered for sale in the slave-market at Rome, asked from what country they came; and being told that they were *Angles* (*Angli*), replied that they ought rather to be called *angels* (*angeli*).

and the meaning equivocal. The passage means probably that Cranmer is actually returned *in his opinions*—in the same opinions which he formerly maintained, supported by the opinions of 'all famous colleges'" (K.). H. thinks that *in* is used for *with*, and that the opinions are those "of learned canonists and divines in Italy and elsewhere," which Cranmer had been sent to collect. I should prefer this explanation to the other if *in*=*with* were found anywhere else.

Almost. On the transposition, see Gr. 420.

Ta'en much pain. Below (v. 1) we have "ta'en some pains." See *Mer.* p. 140.

O' th' inside. See Gr. 175.

The Duchess of Alençon. The daughter of Charles of Orleans, Count of Angoulême, married in 1509 to Charles, Duke of Alençon, who died in 1525. Two years later she was married to Henry d'Albret, King of Navarre. J. H. confounds her with Margaret of Valois, daughter of Henry II. and Catharine de' Medici, and queen to Henry of Navarre, afterwards Henry IV. of France. "The Duchess of Alençon" was the *grandmother* of Henry of Navarre.

There is more in't than fair visage. There is more to be thought of than beauty.

Does whet his anger to him. That is, against him. Cf. *Much Ado*, ii. 1: "The Lady Beatrice hath a quarrel to you." Gr. 187.

Sharp enough, etc. That is, may it be whetted sharp enough, etc.

One Hath crawl'd. One *who* hath, etc. Gr. 244.

Enter the King, reading a schedule. Steevens remarks: "That the cardinal gave the king an inventory of his own private wealth by mistake, and thereby ruined himself, is a known variation from the truth of history. Shakespeare, however, has not injudiciously represented the fall of that great man as owing to an incident which he had once improved to the destruction of another." Holinshed relates this incident as follows:

"Thomas Ruthall, Bishop of Durham, was, after the death of Henry VII., one of the privy council to Henry VIII., to whom the king gave in charge to write a book of the whole estate of the kingdom. Afterwards, the king commanded Cardinal Wolsey to go to this bishop, and to bring the book away with him. This bishop having written two books (the one to answer the king's command, and the other intreating of his own private affairs), did bind them both after one sort in vellum. Now when the cardinal came to demand the book due to the king, the bishop unadvisedly commanded his servant to bring him the book bound in white vellum, lying in his study, in such a place. The servant accordingly brought forth one of the books so bound, being the book intreating of the state of the bishop. The cardinal having the book went from the bishop, and after (in his study by himself) understanding the contents thereof, he greatly rejoiced, having now occasion (which he long sought for) offered unto him, to bring the bishop into the king's disgrace." The result was that the bishop "shortly, through extreme sorrow, ended his life at London, in the year of Christ 1523," and "the cardinal, who had long before gaped after his bishopric," succeeded thereto.

Strikes his breast hard, etc. *Hard* is here a dissyllable. Gr. 485.

Wot. The present tense of *wit* (A. S. *witan*, to know, of which the 1st and 3d persons sing. are *wât*), used some thirty times by S. Cf. *Genesis*, xxi. 26; xxxix. 8; xliv. 15, etc.

Unwittingly. Used only here and in *Rich. III.* ii. 1. We find the verb *unwit* in *Oth.* ii. 3: "As if some planet had unwitted them."

At such proud rate, etc. On so grand a scale that it exceeds what a subject ought to possess.

Withal. "The emphatic form of *with*." See Gr. 196.

Fix'd on spiritual object. The folio reading. The fourth folio has "objects," which Walker and D. adopt.

In your mind. In your memory.

Spiritual leisure. "That is, time devoted to spiritual affairs. *Leisure* seems to be opposed, not to occupation, but to toilsome and compulsory or necessary occupation" (W.). According to Nares, the word "stands simply for space or time allowed." See *Rich. II.* i. 1: "Which then our leisure would not let us hear;" *Rich. III.* v. 3: "The leisure and the fearful time Cuts off," etc.; and again, "The leisure and enforcement of the time Forbids to dwell upon." We still say "I would do it, if leisure permitted," etc. In these instances, "*leisure*" is not precisely "want of leisure," as some explain it, but rather "what leisure I have"—which may be very little.

An ill husband. A bad manager. Cf. *T. of S.* v. 1: "I am undone! While I play the good husband at home, my son and my servant spend all at the University." The word means *husbandman* in 2 *Hen. IV.* v. 3: "he is your servingman and your husband."

Tendance. Attention. Cf. *T. of A.* i. 1: "his love and tendance."

Par'd my present havings. Diminished my wealth. Cf. above, ii. 3: "Our content is our best having."

The prime man. The first man. Cf. *Temp.* i. 2: "My prime request, Which I do last pronounce."

Which went Beyond all man's endeavours. "The sense is, 'My *purposes* went beyond all human *endeavour*. I purposed for your honour more than it falls within the compass of man's nature to attempt'" (Johnson).

Yet fil'd with. That is, kept pace with, came up to. The folio has "fill'd," which no one but Collier believes to be anything else than a misprint.

That ever has and ever shall be. On the ellipsis of *been*, cf. Gr. 395.

The honour of it, etc. "The honour of possessing such a spirit is a reward of its own exercise, as in the contrary case the baseness of a disloyal and disobedient spirit is itself a penal degradation" (J. H.).

Notwithstanding that your bond of duty, etc. "Besides the general bond of duty, by which you are obliged to *be a loyal and obedient subject*, you owe a *particular* devotion of yourself to me as your *particular* benefactor" (Johnson).

That am true and will be. The folio gives this speech as follows:

> "I do professe,
> That for your Highnesse good, I euer labour'd
> More then mine owne: that am, haue, and will be
> (Though all the world should cracke their duty to you,
> And throw it from their Soule, though perils did

> Abound, as thicke as thought could make 'em, and
> Appeare in formes more horrid) yet my Duty,
> As doth a Rocke against the chiding Flood,
> Should the approach of this wilde Riuer breake,
> And stand vnshaken yours."

"The last part of the third line has long been incomprehensible to readers, and unmanageable to editors. Rowe read, 'That am *I*, have *been*, will be.' Mason would have struck the words out. Malone, with some probability, supposed that a line had been lost after 'and will be.' Mr. Singer reads, 'that *I* am *true*, and will be;' and it appears to me that by the latter word, which it will be seen involves but the change of two letters, he has solved the difficulty. But the introduction of '*I*' is needless, as the pronoun occurs twice in the two preceding lines; and under such circumstances the grammar of Shakespeare's time allowed it to be understood. . . . The slight misprint was doubtless assisted by this omission, and the introduction of the long parenthesis—out of place in any case—was a printer's desperate effort to solve the difficulty of the passage. The words 'that am, have, and will be,' might well stand as equivalent to 'that am, have *been*, and will be;' but this would not solve the difficulty; which is to find a subject and a predicate for all these verbs" (W.).

The chiding flood. The sounding, or noisy flood. Cf. *Oth.* ii. 1: "The chiding billow seems to pelt the clouds;" *A. Y. L.* ii. 2: "And churlish chiding of the winter wind;" *M. N. D.* iv. 1: "Never did I hear such gallant chiding" (of hounds), etc.

What should this mean? See Gr. 325.

The story of his anger. The explanation of his anger.

Like a bright exhalation, etc. Like a shooting star.

Enter the Dukes of Norfolk and Suffolk, etc. "Reed remarked that the *Duke of Norfolk*, who is introduced in the first Scene of the first Act, or in 1522, is not the same person who here, or in 1529, demands the great seal from Wolsey; for Thomas Howard, who was created Duke of Norfolk in 1514, died, we are informed by Holinshed, in 1525. And not only are two persons made one, but one, two. For this *Earl of Surrey* is the same who married *Buckingham's* daughter, as we learn from his own lips in the first part of this Scene; and the *Earl of Surrey*, *Buckingham's* son-in-law, is also the very *Duke of Norfolk* who here demands the seals; both titles having been at that time in the family, and he having been summoned to Parliament in 1514 as Earl of Surrey in his own right, his father sitting as Duke of Norfolk. But this supposes a needless complication of blunders. Shakespeare's only error was, probably, ignorance or forgetfulness of the fact that the *Duke of Norfolk*, whom he first brings upon the stage, died before *Wolsey's* fall; and we are to consider *Norfolk* and *Surrey* in this Scene as father and son, and the former as the same person who appears in the first Scene" (W.).

It is a historical fact that Wolsey refused to deliver up the great seal at the demand of the dukes. He retained it until the next day, when they returned with the king's written order for its surrender.

Asher-house. It appears from Holinshed that *Asher* was the ancient name of *Esher*, near Hampton Court. "Shakespeare forgot that Wolsey was himself Bishop of Winchester, unless he meant to say, you must confine yourself to that house which you possess as Bishop of Winchester" (Malone).

Till I find more than will, etc. "Till I find more than will or words (*I mean* more than *your malicious* will and words) to do it—that is, to carry authority so weighty—I will deny to return what the king has given me" (Johnson).

My disgraces. The folio reading. D. has "disgrace;" but the "it" refers to "following my disgraces."

Ye have Christian warrant for them. This is either ironical or sarcastic.

Mine and your master. On *mine*, see Gr. 238.

Letters patents. This is the folio reading, and, as D. remarks, is "according to the phraseology of S.'s time." We find the same form in *Rich. II.* ii. 1, and ii. 3—the only other places where S. uses the expression. Cf. Greene's *James IV.* ii. 1: "your letters-patents," etc.

These forty hours. Malone thought that S. wrote "these four hours;" but, as Steevens remarks, "forty seems anciently to have been the familiar number on many occasions, where no very exact reckoning was necessary." J. H. suggests that "forty hours would have given the cardinal time to take vengeance on Surrey."

Plague of your policy! Cf. 1 *Hen. IV.* ii. 4: "A plague of all cowards!" with *Temp.* i. 1: "A plague upon this howling!" Gr. 175.

Lay upon my credit. Lay to my charge.

Innocent . . . from. Cf. 2 *Hen. VI.* iii. 1: "innocent from meaning treason;" *Macb.* iii. 2: "innocent of the knowledge."

That in the way, etc. Theo. read "That I, in the way," which D. adopts. The meaning may be, *you* that dare mate (match yourself with) *me*, who am a sounder man, etc. Even if we consider "dare" to be in the first person, "that" (relative referring to "I" in "I should tell you") may be its subject, and Theobald's interpolation is needless.

Jaded by a piece of scarlet. Overborne or overmastered by a priest. As in "scarlet sin" above, there is an obvious allusion to the colour of the cardinal's hat and robes.* Cf. 1 *Hen. VI.* i. 3, where Gloster calls Cardinal Beaufort a "scarlet hypocrite."

Dare us with his cap, like larks. "One of the methods of *daring* larks was by small mirrors fastened on scarlet cloth, which engaged the attention of these birds while the fowler drew his net over them" (Steevens). Cf. Greene's *Never too late*, part i.: "They set out their faces as Fowlers do their daring glasses, that the Larkes that soare highest may stoope soonest."

Our issues. Our sons. In the next line the folio has "Whom if he liue," which may be what S. wrote. Cf. Gr. 410.

Fairer And spotless. This may be (as H. makes it) =fairer and more spotless. Cf. *M. of V.* iii. 2: "The best condition'd and unwearied spirit," and note in *Mer.* p. 152. See also Gr. 398.

* Cf. Cavendish's description of Wolsey as he used to go from his house to Westminster Hall: "He came out of his privy chamber, about eight of the clock, appareled all in red; that is to say, his upper garment was either of fine scarlet or taffety, but most commonly of fine crimson satin engrained; his pillion [that is, *cap*] of fine scarlet, with a neck set in the inner side with black velvet, and a tippet of sables about his neck," etc.

You wrought to be a legate, etc. You manœuvred to be one of the pope's legates, and the power you thus gained diminished the jurisdiction of the bishops. As legate, Wolsey took precedence of all other ecclesiastical authorities in the realm.

Ego et rex meus. Holinshed says: "In all writings which he wrote to Rome, or any other foreign prince, he wrote *Ego et rex meus*, I and my king; as who would say that the king were his servant." But, as Wolsey urged in his defence, this order was required by the Latin idiom.

Gregory de Cassalis. The folio has "*de Cassado*," which is probably what S. wrote; following Hall, whose words are: "He, without the king's assent, sent a commission to Sir Gregory de Cassado, knight, to conclude a league between the king and the Duke of Ferrara, without the king's knowledge."

Your holy hat, etc. This charge was made "rather with a view to swell the catalogue than from any serious cause of accusation, inasmuch as the Archbishops Cranmer, Bainbridge, and Warham were indulged with the same privilege" (Douce).

Innumerable substance, etc. Untold treasure, to supply Rome and prepare the way for dignities you seek. *Innumerable* occurs nowhere else in S. Cf. "innumerable treasure" in the quotation from Holinshed below (iv. 2, note on *Of an unbounded stomach*).

The mere undoing. The utter ruin. Cf. *Temp.* p. 111, note on *We are merely cheated.*

'Tis virtue. That is, 'tis virtue to refrain from doing it.

A præmunire. The word *præmunire* is low Latin for *præmonere.* The writ is so called from the first words of it, which *forewarn* the person respecting the offence of introducing foreign authority into England.

Chattels. The folio has "Castles" (not "Cattles," as W. states), which is undoubtedly a misprint; because, as Theo. (who was the first to correct it) remarks, "the judgment in a writ of *præmunire* is, that the defendant shall *be out of the king's protection;* and his *lands* and *tenements, goods* and *chattels*, forfeited to the king; and that his body shall remain in prison at the king's pleasure." This description of the *præmunire* is given by Holinshed, who has "cattels" for "chattels." These forms were then used indifferently; "from which we may infer that the pronunciation was *cattels* in either case" (W.).

Farewell, a long farewell, etc. The punctuation in the folio is, "Farewell? A long farewell to all my Greatnesse." Mr. Jos. Hunter (*New Illust. of S.* vol. ii. p. 108) would retain this, explaining the line thus: "Farewell—did I say Farewell?—Yes, it is too surely so—a long farewell to all my greatness!" But, as D. remarks, "no such recondite meaning was intended here by the author." In the folio we often find the interrogation point where the exclamation point, or some other point, should be used.

The tender leaves of hopes. The folio reading, usually changed to "hope." K. and W. have "hopes," and the latter remarks: "The *s* may be a scribe's or printer's superfluity. But there is an appreciable, though a delicate distinction between 'the tender leaves of hope' and 'the tender leaves of hopes;' and the idea conveyed to me by the latter, of many desires blooming into promise of fruition, is the more beautiful, and is certainly less commonplace."

To-morrow blossoms. Some have thought that *blossoms* is a noun here (and it may be noted that the folio prints it with a capital, "Blossomes"), but it is undoubtedly a verb.

This many summers. Cf. *M. for M.* i. 3: "this nineteen years;" and see Gr. 87.

We would aspire to. Hanmer altered "we" to "he," and has been followed by some editors.

That sweet aspect of princes, and their ruin. On the accent of *aspect*, see *Mer.* p. 128, and cf. below (v. 1): "'Tis his aspect of terror," etc.—*Their ruin* (altered by some editors to "our ruin" or "his ruin") means the ruin which they (princes) cause, or bring; in other words, *their* is a "*subjective* genitive." Similar cases are not rare in S. We have three examples in a single scene (v. 1) of the *Tempest:* "your release," "their high wrongs," and "my wrongs." Cf. *M. N. D.* ii. 1: "Your wrongs (the wrongs done by you) do set a scandal on my sex;" *Lear*, iv. 2: "that their punishment (the punishment inflicted by them) Might have the freer course," etc.

May have a tomb of orphans' tears, etc. The folio reads: "May haue a Tombe of Orphants teares wept on him." The lord chancellor is the general guardian of orphans. Johnson considers the metaphor "very harsh;" but Steevens compares Drummond's *Teares for the Death of Mœliades:*

"The Muses, Phœbus, Love, have raised of their teares
A crystal tomb to him, through which his worth appeares."

He also cites an epigram of Martial's, in which, he says, the Heliades are represented as "weeping a tomb of tears over a viper;" but it is not until after the amber tears of the sisters of Phaëthon have hardened around the reptile (so that he is "concreto vincta gelu") that they are compared to a tomb.

In open. Openly, in public. Steevens considers it a "Latinism," because *in aperto* is used in the same sense; and it is cited as one of the evidences that Ben Jonson "tampered with" this play! It may be noted that "in the open" is now good English (in England, at least) for "in the open air." Cf. Gr. 90.

There was the weight that pulled me down, etc. Cf. what Cavendish says: "Thus passed the cardinal his time forth, from day to day and year to year, in such great wealth, joy, and triumph and glory, having always on his side the king's especial favour, until Fortune, of whose favour no man is longer assured than she is disposed, began to wax something wroth with his prosperous estate. And for the better mean to bring him low, she procured Venus, the insatiate goddess, to be her instrument; who brought the king in love with a gentlewoman that, after she perceived and felt the king's good will towards her, how glad he was to please her, and to grant all her request, wrought the cardinal much displeasure. This gentlewoman was the daughter of Sir Thomas Bullen, knight," etc.

The noble troops that waited, etc. The number of persons who composed Wolsey's household was not less than one hundred and eighty, and some accounts (undoubtedly exaggerated) make it eight hundred. Cf. Cavendish's description of the cardinal's passage through London on his way to France:

"Then marched he forward, from his own house at Westminster, through all London, over London Bridge, having before him a great number of gentlemen, three in a rank, with velvet coats, and the most part of them with great chains of gold about their necks. And all his yeomen followed him, with noblemen's and gentlemen's servants, all in orange-tawny coats, with the cardinal's hat, and a T and a C (for Thomas, Cardinal) embroidered upon all the coats as well of his own servants as all the rest of his gentlemen's servants. And when his sumpter mules, which were twenty or more in number, and all his carriages and carts, and other of his train, were passed before, he rode like a cardinal, very sumptuously, with the rest of his train, on his own mule, with his spare mule and spare horse—trapped in crimson velvet upon velvet, and gilt stirrups—following him. And before him he had two great crosses of silver, his two great pillars* of silver, the king's broad seal of England, and his cardinal's hat, and a gentleman carrying his valence, otherwise called his cloak-bag, which was made of fine scarlet, altogether embroidered very richly with gold, having in it a cloak. Thus passed he forth through London, as I said before; and every day on his journey he was thus furnished, having his harbingers in every place before, which prepared lodging for him and his train."

Make use now. Make interest now. Cf. *M. Ado*, ii. 1: "I gave him use for it;" *V. and A.*: "But gold that's put to use more gold begets;" *Sonn.* 6: "That use is not forbidden usury," etc.

Out of thy honest truth.† See Gr. 168.

Dull cold marble. Cf. Gray, *Elegy*: "the dull cold ear of death."

Must be heard of. See Gr. 424.

Cherish those hearts that hate thee. Warburton thought that S. did not mean to make Wolsey so good a Christian as this would imply, and that he probably wrote "cherish those hearts that *wait* thee," that is, thy dependants!

Still in thy right hand, etc. There may be an allusion here, as some have thought, to "the rod of silver with the dove," or "bird of peace," carried at royal processions. See below (v. 1) in the *Order of the Procession*, and also in the account of the coronation that follows.

Had I but served my God, etc. It is a historical fact that, among his last words to Sir William Kingston, the cardinal said, "If I had served God as diligently as I have done the king, he would not have given me over in my gray hairs. But this is the just reward that I must receive for my diligent pains and study that I have had to do him service, not regarding my service to God, but only to satisfy his pleasure."

* On these *pillars*, see above, notes on stage direction at beginning of ii. 4.

† Cromwell remained with Wolsey during his confinement at Esher, and obtained a seat in Parliament that he might defend him there. The Lords passed a bill of impeachment against the cardinal, but Cromwell opposed it in the Commons with such skill and eloquence that he finally defeated it. "At the length," says Cavendish, "his honest estimation and earnest behaviour in his master's cause, grew so in every man's opinion, that he was reputed the most faithful servant to his master of all other, wherein he was greatly of all men commended."

ANNE BULLEN.

ACT IV.

SCENE I.—The ceremonies attending the coronation of Anne Bullen are minutely described by Hall, from whom S. drew the materials for this scene, including the "Order of the Procession." Sir Thomas More was the chancellor on this occasion.

Their royal minds. Their loyal dispositions. Cf. 2 *Hen. IV.* iv. 1: "our royal faiths" (altered by Hanmer to "loyal faiths"). In the present instance, however, the word may mean *noble* (Steevens) or *generous* (H.).

Better taken. Better received, more heartily welcomed.

Of those that claim their offices, etc. Holinshed says: "In the beginning of May, 1533, the king caused open proclamation to be made, that all men that claimed to do any service, or execute any office, at the solemn feast of the coronation, by the way of tenure, grant, or prescription, should put their grant, three weeks after Easter, in the Star Chamber, before Charles, Duke of Suffolk, for that time high steward of England, and the lord chancellor, and other commissioners."

Dunstable, six miles off From Ampthill. The court was held at Dunstable Priory, which was a royal foundation of Henry I., who in 1131 bestowed on it the town of Dunstable and all its privileges. Ampthill Castle, built in the fifteenth century, was one of the favourite resorts of Henry VIII. It was demolished about the year 1626. After many changes of proprietorship, the estate came into the possession of Lord Ossory, who planted a grove of firs where the castle had stood, and in 1773 erected in the centre a monument, surmounted by a cross bearing a shield with Katherine's arms, of Castile and Arragon. A tablet at the base of the cross bears the following inscription, from the pen of Horace Walpole:

"In days of yore, here Ampthill's towers were seen,
The mournful refuge of an injur'd queen;
Here flow'd her pure but unavailing tears,
Here blinded zeal sustain'd her sinking years.
Yet Freedom hence her radiant banner wav'd,
And Love aveng'd a realm by priests enslav'd;
From Catherine's wrongs a nation's bliss was spread,
And Luther's light from lawless Henry's bed."

Where the princess lay. That is, where she resided. Cf. *T. N.* iii. 1: "So thou mayst say, the king lies by a beggar, if a beggar dwell near him;" *M.W.* ii. 2: "When the court lay at Windsor;" 1 *Hen. VI.* ii. 2: "To visit her poor castle where she lies." So also in Milton, *L'Allegro:* "Where perhaps some beauty lies," etc.

The late marriage. "The marriage lately considered as a valid one" (Steevens); or simply the *previous* marriage.

Kimbolton. The folio has "Kymmalton," which was doubtless the pronunciation of the name. Kimbolton Castle, in Huntingdonshire, successively the property of the Bohuns, the Staffords, and the Wingfields, is now the seat of the Duke of Manchester. From an interesting account of the place in the *Athenæum* (Jan. 1861), I extract a paragraph or two:

"Kimbolton is perhaps the only house now left in England in which you still live and move, distinguished as the scene of an act in one of Shakespeare's plays. Where now is the royal palace of Northampton? Where the baronial hall of Warkworth? . . . The Tower has become a barrack, and Bridewell a jail. . . . Westminster Abbey, indeed, remains much as when Shakespeare opened the great contention of York and Lancaster with the dead hero of Agincourt lying there in state; and the Temple Gardens have much the same shape as when he made Plantagenet pluck the white rose, Somerset the red; but for a genuine Shakespearian house, in which men still live and move, still dress and dine, to which guests come and go, in which children frisk and sport, where shall we look beyond the walls of Kimbolton Castle?

"Of this Shakespearian pile Queen Katherine is the glory and the fear. The chest in which she kept her clothes and jewels, her own cipher on the lid, still lies at the foot of the grand staircase, in the gallery leading to the seat she occupied in the private chapel. Her spirit, the people of the castle say, still haunts the rooms and corridors in the dull gloaming or at silent midnight. . . . Mere dreams, no doubt; but people here believe them. They say the ghost glides about after dark, robed in her long white dress, and with the royal crown upon her head, through the great hall, and along the corridor to the private chapel, or up the grand staircase, past the Pellegrini cartoons."

The Order of the Procession. Called in the folio "The Order of the

Coronation;" but it is only the procession on the return from the coronation. W. remarks: "This elaborate direction is of no service to the action, and was plainly intended only for the prompter and property-man of the theatre, that in getting up this show play they might have exact directions about putting this Scene on the stage. But as it doubtless gives us a very exact measure of the capacity of our old theatre to present a spectacle, it should be retained." The direction for the exit of the procession follows the "Order" in these words: "Exeunt, *first passing ouer the Stage in Order and State, and then, A great Flourish of Trumpets.*"

Choristers. "Quirristers" in the folio.

Then Garter. Garter king at arms, in his coat of office emblazoned with the royal arms.

Collars of SS. The folio has "*Esses.*" "A collar of *SS*, probably so called from the S-shaped links of the chain-work, was a badge of equestrian nobility."

Four of the Cinque-ports. The *Cinque Ports*, on the south coast of England, were originally *five* (hence the name)—Dover, Hastings, Hythe, Romney, and Sandwich: Winchelsea and Rye were afterwards added. They were under the jurisdiction of barons, called wardens, for the better security of the coast, these ports being nearest to France, and considered the keys of the kingdom. The office was instituted by William the Conqueror in 1078. The Duke of Wellington was lord-warden from 1828 to his death in 1852 (cf. Longfellow's poem, "The Warden of the Cinque Ports").

On each side her. Cf. *L. L. L.* v. 2: "writ o' both sides the leaf." Gr. 202.

Her hair richly adorned. The folio has "*in her haire*," etc.; an error probably occasioned by "in her robe" immediately preceding.

I' th' abbey. That is, Westminster Abbey.

The mere rankness. The very exuberance. See above (iii. 2) on *The mere undoing*, and cf. Gr. 15.

The choicest music. The best musicians. See *Mer.* p. 162.

So she parted. See *Mer.* p. 145, note on *Part.*

Newly preferr'd. Just promoted. See *Mer.* p. 140.

Something I can command. That is, I can do something for your entertainment.

SCENE II.—*But I think your grace.* The folio has "I thanke," etc.; a misprint corrected in the second folio.

Happily. Haply; as often in S. See Gr. 42.

The stout earl Northumberland. See p. 34, foot-note.

At York. Wolsey had removed to his see of York, by the king's command, and had taken up his residence at Cawood Castle (ten miles from the city), which belonged to the Archbishops of York. There he rendered himself extremely popular in the neighbourhood by his affability and hospitality.

With easy roads. "The king," said Cavendish to Wolsey, "hath sent gentle Master Kingston to convey you by such easy journeys as you will command him to do." On *with*, see Gr. 193.

To Leicester. "The next day," says Cavendish, "we rode to Leicester

YORK CATHEDRAL.

Abbey; and by the way he waxed so sick that he was divers times likely to have fallen from his mule; and being night before we came to the Abbey of Leicester, where at his coming in at the gates, the abbot of the place, with all his convent, met him with the light of many torches; whom

LEICESTER ABBEY.

they right honourably received with great reverence. To whom my lord said, 'Father abbot, I am come hither to leave my bones among you.'"

Leicester Abbey was founded in the year 1143, in the reign of King Stephen, by Robert Bossu, Earl of Leicester, and was dedicated to the Virgin Mary. It is situated in a pleasant meadow to the north of the town, watered by the River Soar, whence it acquired the name of *St. Mary de Pratis*, or *de la Pré*.

The remains of Wolsey were interred in the abbey church, and were attended to the grave by the abbot and all his brethren. This last ceremony was performed by torchlight, the canons singing dirges and offering orisons, between four and five o'clock on the morning of St. Andrew's Day, November 30th, 1530. There is a traditional story that the stone coffin in which the remains were placed was, after its disinterment, used as a horse-trough at an inn near Leicester.

With all his covent. The folio has "his Couent," and in *M. for M.* iv. 3, "One of our Couent." D., who gives "covent" in both passages, remarks that this is a very old form of *convent.* He quotes the ballad, *A Lytell Geste of Robyn Hode:*

> "The abbot sayd to his covent,
> There he stode on grounde," etc.

He might have added that we still have the old form in "Covent Garden" (in London), which was originally the garden of the *convent* at Westminster.

Of an unbounded stomach. Of unbounded pride, or *arrogance.* See *Temp.* p. 115.

In this character of Wolsey the poet follows Holinshed very closely: "This cardinal (as you may perceive in this story) was of a great stomach, for he counted himself equal with princes, and by crafty suggestion gat into his hands innumerable treasure: he forced* little on simony, and was not pitiful, and stood affectionate in his own opinion: in open presence he would lie and say untruth, and was double both in speech and meaning: he would promise much and perform little: he was vicious of his body, and gave the clergy evil example."

By suggestion Tith'd all the kingdom. The folio has "Ty'de all the Kingdome." As the clause is the counterpart of Holinshed's "by crafty suggestion gat into his hands innumerable treasure," it is probable that "ty'de" is a misprint for "ty'thde." Hanmer was the first to make the correction, and is followed by Sr., D., and W. K. and H. retain "tied;" but the former has "no doubt that the allusion is to the acquisition of wealth by the cardinal," and the latter admits that Wolsey's "general course and history make rather in behalf of" the other reading. "By suggestion tied all the kingdom" is explained as meaning, "by craft limited, or infringed the liberties of the kingdom."

I' th' presence. In the royal presence.

Men's evil manners, etc. Cf. *J. C.* iii. 2:

> "The evil that men do lives after them;
> The good is oft interred with their bones."

* That is, hesitated, or had scruples. Cf. *L. L. L.* v. 2: "You force not to forswear."

The *Var.* ed. gives several quotations from old writers, closely resembling the passage in the text; as from Whitney's *Emblemes* (1586):

"*Scribit in marmore læsus.*
In marble harde our harmes wee always grave,
Because, we still will beare the same in minde:
In duste wee write the benefittes we have,
Where they are soone defaced with the winde," etc.

This cardinal, etc. This speech also follows Holinshed: "This cardinal (as Edmund Campian, in his history of Ireland, describeth him) was a man undoubtedly born to honour: I think (saith he) some prince's bastard, no butcher's son, exceeding wise, fair spoken, high minded, full of revenge, vicious of his body; lofty to his enemies, were they never so big, to those that accepted and sought his friendship wonderful courteous; a ripe schoolman, thrall to affections, brought a-bed with flattery; insatiable to get, and more princely in bestowing; as appeareth by his two colleges at Ipswich and Oxenford, the one overthrown with his fall, the other unfinished, and yet, as it lieth, for an house of students incomparable throughout Christendom. . . . A great preferrer of his servants, an advancer of learning, stout in every quarrel, never happy till his overthrow; wherein he showed such moderation, and ended so perfectly, that the hour of his death did him more honour than all the pomp of his life passed."

Was fashion'd to much honour, etc. The folio points thus:

"Was fashion'd to much Honor. From his Cradle
He was a Scholler, and a ripe, and good one," etc.

Exceeding wise. See *Mer.* p. 128, note on *Exceeding strange.*

Oxford. It was Christ Church College that Wolsey founded.

The good that did it. "The goodness that founded it." Pope read "the good he did it;" Collier's MS. corrector, "the good man that did it;" St. has "the good that rear'd it." K., D., W., and H. follow the folio.

Cause the musicians play. See Gr. 349, and cf. below, "I caus'd you write."

Solemnly tripping. "*Trip* signified a dancing kind of motion, either light or serious" (Keightley).

Vizards. Visors, masks. Cf. *M. W.* iv. 4: "I'll go buy them vizards;" *Macb.* iii. 2: "make our faces vizards to our hearts." We find also *vizarded*, as in *M. W.* iv. 6: "masked and vizarded."

Bid the music leave. See above (iv. 1) on *The choicest music.*

An earthy cold. The *Var.* ed. and H. have "earthly;" Sr., Walker, and D., "earthy colour;" Collier's MS. corrector, "earthy coldness."

Deserve we no more reverence? On Katherine's refusal to give up the title of queen, see *Introduction*, pp. 31, 34.

Capucius. The Latin form of *Chapuys.* See p. 35.

That letter I caus'd you write. The letter given on page 35.

Model. Image, representative. Cf. *A. W.* iv. 3: "this counterfeit model;" *Rich. II.* i. 2:

"In that thou seest thy wretched brother die,
Who was the model of thy father's life."

Let him be a noble. Even though he should be a nobleman. Some editors put a semicolon after "husband."

They are the poorest. On *the*, see Gr. 92.
I can no more. See Gr. 307.

ACT V.

SCENE I.—*These should be hours.* On *hours*, see Gr. 480.

At primero. A game at cards, very fashionable in that day. Cf. *M. W.* iv. 5: "I never prospered since I forswore myself at primero." Some of the technicalities of the game, as given in Minsheu's *Dialogues in Spanish and English* (quoted by D.), were very similar to those in certain games now in vogue; as "Passe," "I am come to passe againe," "Ile see it," "I am flush," etc.

Some touch of your late business. "Some hint of the business that keeps you awake so late" (Johnson).

In great extremity; and fear'd. On the ellipsis, see Gr. 403.

Mine own way. "Mine own opinion in religion" (Johnson).

Is made master, etc. The folio reading, altered by Theo. to "he's made master." For the ellipsis, see Gr. 400.

The gap and trade, etc. "*Trade* is the *practised method*, the *general course*" (Johnson). Steevens compares *Rich. II.* iii. 3: "Some way of common trade." So *traded* sometimes means *practised, experienced;* as in *T. and C.* ii. 2: "Two traded pilots 'twixt the dangerous shores."

Sir, I may tell it you, etc. I have adopted Dyce's pointing here. The folio has

> "and indeed this day,
> Sir (I may tell it you) I think I haue
> Incenst the Lords o' th' Councell," etc.

Incens'd the lords. According to Nares, *incense* (or *insense*) means "to instruct, inform; a provincial expression still quite current in Staffordshire, and probably Warwickshire, whence we may suppose S. had it." Cf. *M. Ado*, v. 1: "how Don John, your brother, incensed me to slander the lady Hero." This interpretation is adopted by V., W., and H. K. prints "insensed," without comment.

Have broken with the king. That is, have communicated with, have broached the subject to him. Cf. *T. G. of V.* iii. 1: "I am to break with thee of some affairs;" *M. Ado*, i. 1: "I will break with her"—and in several other places in the same play. See also *M. Wives*, iii. 2; *J. C.* ii. 1; *K. John*, iv. 2; etc. S. nowhere uses the phrase in the modern sense of *quarrel with.*

Convented. Summoned. Cf. *M. for M.* v. 1: "Whensoever he's convented;" *Cor.* ii. 2: "We are convented Upon a pleasing treaty."

Is she crying out? Is she in labour?

The estate of my poor queen. On *estate*, see *Mer.* p. 151.

Enter Sir Anthony Denny. Denny was one of the companions of Henry's younger days, knighted about the year 1541, and made one of the privy council.

Avoid the gallery. Clear the gallery. See *Temp.* p. 137.

With such freedom purge yourself. Clear yourself so completely.

You a brother of us. "You being one of the council, it is necessary to imprison you, that the witnesses against you may not be deterred" (Johnson). Cf. what Suffolk says in the next scene: "you are a counsellor," etc. Gr. 381.

Throughly. See *Mer.* p. 144, note on *Throughfares.*

By my holy dame. By the Virgin; like "God's blest mother!" below. The folio has "Holydame," which D. takes to be "halidom." The latter is found in *T. G. of V.* iv. 2—"By my halidom, I was fast asleep!"—and was a common oath in that day. The word is probably from the A. S. *hâlig*, holy, and the suffix *dom* (as in *freedom*, *kingdom*, etc.), and means "holiness," or "sacred oath" (Wb.).

According to Fox, Henry said, "Oh Lorde, what maner o' man be you? What simplicitie is in you? I had thought that you would rather have sued to us to have taken the paines to have heard you and your accusers together for your triall, without any such indurance."

Indurance. Being put in durance; imprisonment. S. uses the word nowhere else, taking it here from Fox.

The good I stand on. The advantage, or merit, in which I trust. This is the folio reading, for which Johnson proposed to substitute "The ground I stand on;" a plausible emendation, made also by Collier's MS. corrector, and adopted by W. K., D., and H. retain "good."

I weigh not. I value not. Cf. *L. L. L.* v. 2: "You weigh me not? O that's, you care not for me."

I fear nothing. Here *nothing* is an adverb. Gr. 55.

Know you not, etc. Cf. Fox: "Do you not know what state you be in with the whole world, and how many great enemies you have? Do you not consider what an easie thing it is to procure three or foure false knaves to witness against you? Thinke you to have better lucke that waie than your master Christ had? I see by it you will run headlong to your undoing, if I would suffer you," etc.

Not ever. That is, not always; it is *not* equivalent to *never.*

Might corrupt knaves, etc. On the accent of *corrupt*, cf. Gr. 475, 476.

Ween you. Do you think, or imagine? Cf. 1 *Hen. VI.* ii. 5: "weening to redeem"—the only instance of the word given by Mrs. Clarke, the one in the text being omitted.

Perjur'd witness. Perjured testimony. D. prints it "witness'," as if a contraction of "witnesses." See Gr. 471, and *Temp.* p. 116, note on *Made thee more profit Than other princess can.*

Whiles. See *Mer.* p. 133.

Naughty earth. Wicked earth. See *Mer.* p. 152.

A precipice. The folio has "a Precepit," and in the next line "woe" for "woo;" both corrected in second folio.

Enter an old Lady. "It is painful to think that Steevens was probably correct in his irreverent supposition that 'this is the same old cat that appears with Anne Bullen' in a previous Scene" (W.).

Now, good angels, etc. Cf. *Ham.* iii. 4:

> "Save me, and hover o'er me with your wings,
> You heavenly guards!"

And of a lovely boy, etc. "The humour of the passage consists in the talkative old lady, who had in her hurry said it was a boy, adding 'bless *her*' before she corrects her mistake" (Boswell).

Desires your visitation, etc. Desires you to visit her and to be acquainted, etc. Cf. Gr. 356. On *visitation*, see *Temp*. p. 130.

SCENE II.—*Doctor Butts*. "Sir William Butts, principal physician to Henry VIII., and one of the founders of the College of Physicians, was a man of great learning and judgment" (J. H.).

Sound not my disgrace. That is, proclaim it. Cf. *K. John*, iv. 2:

"Then I, as one that am the tongue of these,
To sound the purposes of all their hearts," etc.

I never sought their malice. I never gave occasion for their malice.

Wait else. See Gr. 420.

Enter the King and Butts at a window above. "In America we are not without some examples of old houses in which large rooms are commanded by windows opening into them from passage-ways or small adjacent apartments. But of old it was quite common in England to have such windows in the large rooms of manor halls, castles, and palaces, especially in the kitchen and the dining-room, or banqueting-hall. From these apertures the mistress of the mansion could overlook the movements of her servants, either with or without their knowledge, and direct them without the trouble and unpleasantness of mingling with them. Instead of a window, there was very often a door opening upon a small gallery or platform, not unlike those in which the musicians are placed in some assembly rooms. Such a gallery, too, was part of the stage arrangement of Shakespeare's day" (W.).

They had parted, etc. "They had *shared;* that is, had so much honesty among them" (Steevens).

The Council Chamber. "Theobald, the first regulator of Shakespeare's plays, should have begun a new Scene here, although the stage direction in the folio is only '*A Councell Table brought in with Chayres and Stooles, and placed vnder the State*,' etc. But this is plainly the mere result of the absence of scenery of any kind on Shakespeare's stage, and the audience were to imagine that the Scene changed from the lobby before the Council Chamber to that apartment itself. For it will be observed that *Cranmer*, entering the former, finds the doors of the latter shut ('all fast') against him: he is bidden to enter, and the king and Dr. Butts afterward do enter the Council Chamber, according to the direction of the folio. It is true that the *Door-keeper* appears in both Scenes; but in the former he is within, in the latter he is summoned from without. This must be regarded, of course, in the performance of the play before a modern audience; but as the Scene has remained undivided until the present day, except by those early editors who followed the French custom of making a new Scene at every important entrance or exit, a rectification of the slight want of conformity to mere external truth would not compensate for the inconvenience to those who refer to the play consequent upon a disturbance of the old arrangement" (W.). The Camb. editors begin a new scene here.

Enter the Lord Chancellor. On the 29th of November, 1529, Sir Thomas

More received the great seal, surrendered by Wolsey on the 18th of the same month. As he in turn surrendered it on the 16th of May, 1532, which was before the date of this scene as fixed by the mention of the birth of Elizabeth (September 7th, 1533), Theo. argues that Sir Thomas Audley, More's successor, must be the chancellor meant here. He was, however (as Malone remarks), lord keeper at this time, and did not obtain the title of Chancellor until the January after the birth of Elizabeth. For the purposes of the *drama*, it would be better to consider More as the chancellor here, his appointment to the office having been mentioned in the preceding act; but as a matter of *history*, Audley held the great seal in 1543, when Cranmer was accused of heresy. As has been stated in the *Introduction* (p. 15), S. here brings into one scene events separated by an interval of at least ten years.

At this present. This old phrase, now used only in the language of the law, is found occasionally in S.; as in *W. T.* i. 2, etc. We find also "for this present," in *J. C.* i. 2; "on the present," in *T. of A.* i. 1; "in present," in *T. and C.* iii. 2 and 3, etc. Bacon uses "at that present" (in his *Hen. VII.*) in a similar way.

Capable Of our flesh. "Liable to, or capable of, the weaknesses belonging to flesh and blood" (V.); "susceptible of fleshly temptations" (St.); "capable of the sins of our flesh" (W.). K. and D. also retain this folio reading. Pope read "and capable Of frailty;" Malone, "In our own natures frail, incapable; Of our flesh, few are angels;" Mason, "frail and culpable," with Malone's pointing; Collier's MS. corrector (followed by H.), "culpable Of our flesh."

Pace them not in their hands. Do not lead them about.

Manage. See *Mer.* p. 153.

The upper Germany. "Alluding to the heresy of Thomas Münzer, which sprung up in Saxony in the years 1521 and 1522" (Grey).

A single heart. A heart free from duplicity. Cf. *Acts*, ii. 46.

Stirs against. Bestirs himself, or is active against. Collier's MS. corrector has "strives against;" but cf. *Rich. II.* i. 2: "To stir against the butchers of his life."

A public peace. Rowe (and Collier's MS. corrector) read "the public peace," which D. adopts.

Men that make Envy and crooked malice nourishment. Cf. above (iii. 2), "How eagerly ye follow my disgraces, As if it fed ye!"

Be what they will. Whoever they may be. Gr. 254, 400. Cf. *Lear*, v. 3:

> "What in the world he is
> That names me traitor, villain-like he lies."

By that virtue. By virtue of that office.

I shall both find. On the transposition, see Gr. 420.

Your painted gloss, etc. "Those that understand you, under this *painted gloss*, this fair outside, discover your empty talk and your false reasoning" (Johnson).

This is too much. The folio gives this speech to the chamberlain, and also the ones beginning "Then thus for you" and "'Tis now too certain." The misprint of "*Cham.*" for "*Chan.*" is easily made. "This is the king's ring" probably belongs to the chamberlain, who appears to speak only this once during the scene.

Such flattery now. Pope (followed by D.) read "flatteries;" but "they" in the next line may refer to "commendations." I adopt D.'s pointing.

Thin and bare. The folio has "thin, and base." The correction is Malone's, and is adopted by D., V., W., and H.

To me you cannot reach, etc. The folio has a comma at the end of the preceding line, and points this line thus: "To me you cannot reach. You play the Spaniell," which most of the editors retain. Mason suggested the reading in the text, and is followed by D. and the Cambridge editors. See Gr. 244.

Than but once think this place. The folio has "his place." Rowe made the correction, which is generally adopted. K. retains "his."

I had thought I had had. I thought I had. Cf. Gr. 360. According to Fox, the king said, "Ah, my lords, I thought I had wiser men of my counsaile than now I find you. What discretion was this in you thus to make the primate of the realme, and one of you in office, to wait at the counsaille-chamber doore amongst servingmen? You might have considered that he was a counsailer as wel as you, and you had no such commission of me so to handle him. I was content that you should trie him as a counsellor, and not as a meane subject. But now I well perceive that things be done against him maliciouslie, and if some of you might have had your mindes, you would have tried him to the uttermost. But I doe you all to wit, and protest, that if a prince may bee beholding unto his subject (and so solemnlie laying his hand upon his brest, said), by the faith I owe to God, I take this man here, my lord of Canterburie, to be of all other a most faithful subject unto us, and one to whome we are much beholding, giving him great commendations otherwise."

Had ye mean. S. commonly uses the plural *means*, but has *mean* in several instances; as in *J. C.* iii. 1: "no mean of death;" *A. and C.* iv. 6: "a swifter mean;" *T. A.* ii. 5: "that mean;" *Oth.* iii. 1: "I'll devise a mean," etc. Cf. Bacon, *Essay* xix.: "thinke to Command the End, and not to endure the Meane," etc.

What was purpos'd Concerning his imprisonment, etc. "And with that," says Fox, "one or two of the chiefest of the counsaile, making their excuse, declared, that in requesting his indurance, it was rather ment for his triall and his purgation against the common fame and slander of the worlde, than for any malice conceived against him. 'Well, well, my lords (quoth the king), take him, and well use him, as hee is worthy to bee, and make no more ado.' And with that, every man caught him by the hand, and made faire weather of altogethers, which might easilie be done with that man."

That is, a fair young maid. Rowe read "There is," which D. and W. favour. We may explain it, as it stands, by Gr. 414. Cf. *R. and J.* iv. 2: "this reverend holy friar, All our whole city is much bound to him." Or we may assume an ellipsis of "to" after "godfather;" and compare above (ii. 1):

—"whoever the king favours,
The cardinal instantly will find employment" (for).

You'd spare your spoons. It was the old custom for the sponsors at christening to make a present of gilt spoons to the child. These were called *apostle spoons*, because figures of the apostles were carved on the handles. Rich people gave the whole twelve, but those who were poorer or more penurious limited themselves to four (for the evangelists), or even to one, which represented the patron saint of the child. Allusions to these spoons are frequent in our old writers. The *Var.* ed. fills a page with examples.

This line and the two that follow are printed as prose in the folio (so in W., H., and Cambridge ed.), but, as Abbott remarks (Gr. 333), this "makes an extraordinary and inexplicable break in a scene which is wholly verse." See also remarks on proper names in the metre of S. on p. 354 of Gr.

Thy true heart. The folio has "hearts;" corrected in second folio.

A shrewd turn. An ill turn. See *Mer.* p. 151, or C. pp. 221–224.

Trifle time away. Cf. *M. of V.* iv. 1: "We trifle time."

Made a Christian. That is, christened.

THE BEAR GARDEN.

SCENE III.—*Parish Garden.* The vulgar pronunciation of *Paris Garden.* "This celebrated bear-garden on the Bankside was so called from

Robert de Paris, who had a house and garden there in the time of Richard II." (Malone.) The Globe Theatre stood on the southern side of the Thames, and was contiguous to this garden, which was noted for its noise and disorder.

Gaping. "Shouting or roaring. Littleton's Dict. has 'To gape or bawl, *vociferor*'" (Reed). This may be the meaning of the word in *M. of V.* iv. 1: "a gaping pig."

May-day morning. All ranks of people used to "go a Maying" on the first of May. Stowe says: "In the month of May, namely, on May-day in the morning, every man, except impediment, would walk into the sweet meadows and green woods; there to rejoice their spirits with the beauty and savour of sweet flowers, and with the noise* of birds, praising God in their kind."

We read in Hall of the Venetian ambassadors, in 1515, accompanying Queen Katherine, in great state, to meet Henry VIII. at Shooter's Hill, near Greenwich; and, after music and a banquet, they proceeded homeward; certain pasteboard giants (Gog and Magog) being borne in the procession, and "Lincoln green" worn in honour of Robin Hood. Katherine also gathered "May-dew" in Greenwich Park.

Paul's. St. Paul's Cathedral. It is "Powles" in the folio, as often; "but this is a mere phonographic irregularity, not a characteristic vulgarism like 'Parish' above. 'Paul' was universally pronounced *Pole* in S.'s time" (W.).

Four foot. Cf. 1 *Hen. IV.* ii. 2: "four foot;" *W. T.* iv. 3: "twelve foot and a half," etc. So "three pound of sugar" (*W. T.* iv. 2), "a hundred pound in gold" (*M. W.* iv. 6), etc. This use of the singular for the plural in familiar terms of weight and measure is common even now in vulgar speech.

Sir Guy nor Colbrand. Sir Guy of Warwick was a famous hero of the old romances, and Colbrand was a Danish giant whom he subdued at Winchester.

Let me ne'er hope to see a chine again, etc. This passage stands thus in the folio:

> "Let me ne're hope to see a Chine againe,
> And that I would not for a Cow, God saue her."

Collier's MS. corrector altered "chine" to "queen," and "cow" to "crown;" but, as Lettsom remarks, "he seems to have been confounding in his memory the christening procession of the next scene with the coronation procession of iv. 1." As the former took place on the fourth day after the birth of the princess, it is pretty certain that the queen could not have been present. The main difficulty in the passage has been the "God save her!" as referring to "cow;" but a writer in the *Literary Gazette* (Jan. 25, 1862) says that a phrase identical with that used by Shakespeare is in use to this day in the south of England. "'Oh! I would not do that for a

* *Noise* sometimes meant chorus, symphony, music, or band of musicians. Cf. 2 *Hen. IV.* ii. 4: "See if thou canst find out Sneak's noise: Mistress Tearsheet would fain have some music;" Spenser, *F. Q.* i. 12, 39: "During the which there was an heavenly noise;" Milton, *At a Solemn Music*: "that melodious noise;" *Hymn on Nativity*: "the stringed noise," etc. We find this meaning as far back as Chaucer; as in *The Flower and Leafe*: "it was a blisful noise to here."

cow, save her tail!' may still be heard in the mouths of the vulgar in Devonshire." St. quotes Greene and Lodge's *Looking Glasse for London* (1598): "my blind mare, God bless her!" On the whole, we may assume that the old reading is the right one, and that the porter's man was thinking, not of a queen, but of a chine of beef.

Moorfields. "The train-bands of the city were exercised in Moorfields" (Johnson).

Under the line. Under the equator. See the same phrase in *Temp.* iv. 1.

Brazier. A brass-founder, and a small portable furnace. "Both these senses are understood" (Johnson).

Fire-drake. The word has several meanings: a fiery dragon (as in the Romance of Bevis of Hampton), a will-o'-the-wisp, or *ignis fatuus*, and "a firework which sprang fitfully about in the air with many explosions."

Pink'd porringer. Pinked means "worked in eyelet holes." Compare *T. of S.* iv. 3:

> "*Haberdasher.* Here is the cap your worship did bespeak.
> *Petruchio.* Why, this was moulded on a porringer;
> * * * * * * *
> Away with it! come let me have a bigger.
> *Katherine.* I'll have no bigger: this doth fit the time,
> And gentlewomen wear such caps as these."

The meteor. The "fire-drake."

Clubs. This was the rallying cry of the London apprentices, who used their clubs to preserve the public peace; but sometimes, as here, to raise a disturbance (D.). Cf. 1 *Hen. IV.* i. 3: "I'll call for clubs, if you will not away." S. often puts home phrases into the mouths of foreign characters, and we find this one in *T. A.* ii. 1, *R. and J.* i. 1, etc.

To the broomstaff to me. Pope and Collier's MS. corrector read "with me;" but cf. "a quarrel to you" (*M. Ado*, ii. 1), and see Gr. 185–190.

Loose shot. Random shooters.

Win the work. Carry the fortification.

The Tribulation of Tower Hill or the limbs of Limehouse. "No other allusion to these places or assemblages has been discovered. It may be that these are the names of Puritan congregations, and that S. meant a satirical fling at the pretended meekness of that body; but it may also be that 'their dear brothers' refers to the obstreperous youths first named, and that the 'audiences' referred to were of the same kidney. Within the memory of men now living 'Tribulation' was a common name among New England families of Puritan descent" (W.).

Limbo Patrum. "In confinement. 'In limbo' continues to be a cant phrase, in the same sense, at this day" (Malone). The *Limbus Patrum* is properly "the purgatory of the Patriarchs," where they are supposed to be waiting for the resurrection. Cf. *C. of E.* iv. 2: "he's in Tartar Limbo, worse than hell;" *T. A.* iii. 1: "as far from help as Limbo is from bliss;" *A. W.* v. 3: "of Satan, and of Limbo," etc.

A running banquet. The word *banquet* used to mean, not the full dinner or supper, but merely the *dessert.* Cf. Massinger, *Unnatural Combat*, iii. 1:

> "We'll *dine* in the great room; but let the music
> And *banquet* be prepared here."

So in Cavendish's *Life of Wolsey:* "where they did both sup and banquet." In this case, a whipping was to be the *dessert* of the rioters after their regular course of *Limbo.*

Baiting of bombards. That is, tippling. See *Temp.* p. 128.

Torn a pieces. See Gr. 24 and 140.

A Marshalsea. The Marshalsea was a well-known prison.

Get up o' the rail. Mason would read "off the rail;" but *of* was often used where we should use *from.* See Gr. 166. We still say "out of the house," etc.

I'll pick you. The folio has "Ile pecke you." Cf. *Cor.* i. 1: "as high As I could pick my lance;" where, as here, *pick* (or *peck,* which is the same word) means *pitch.*

CHRISTENING GIFTS.

SCENE IV.—*The Palace.* At Greenwich, where, as we learn from Hall, this procession was made from the Church of the Friars.

Standing bowls. Bowls elevated on feet or pedestals. See the cut above. According to Hall (whom S. follows in the account of the christening), "the Archbishop of Canterbury gave to the princess a standing cup of gold; the Duchess of Norfolk gave to her a standing cup of gold, fretted with pearl; the Marchioness of Dorset gave three gilt bowls, pounced, with a cover; and the Marchioness of Exeter gave three standing bowls, graven, all gilt, with a cover."

Gossips. A *gossip,* in its first and etymological sense, as Trench (*Select Glossary,* etc.) remarks, "is a sponsor in baptism—one *sib* or akin in *God,* according to the doctrine of the mediæval Church, that sponsors contracted a spiritual affinity with one another, with the parents, and with the child itself. 'Gossips,' in this primary sense, would ordinarily be intimate and familiar with one another, . . . and thus the word was next applied to all familiars and intimates. At a later day it obtained the meaning which is now predominant in it, namely, the idle profitless talk, the *commérage* (which word has exactly the same history) that too often finds place in the intercourse of such."

Cf. *C. of E.* v. 1: "Go to a gossip's feast;" *W.T.* ii. 3: "needful conference About some gossips for your highness," etc.

Saba. The folio reading. "Except in the translations of the Bible the word 'Sheba' seems to have been unknown to English and even to Latin literature in the time of Shakespeare. Solomon's dusky admirer was Queen of Sheba; but in the Septuagint, as well as in the Latin Vulgate, she herself is called Saba: Καὶ βασίλισσα Σαβὰ ἤκουσε τὸ ὄνομα Σαλωμών. 1 *Kings*, x. 1" (W.). I take it that Σαβά here is the name of the country, and not of the queen. The Arab legends (which are mere legends, of course) call her Balkis. In Peele and Marlowe, as in S., she is spoken of as "Saba."

Under his own vine. Cf. *Micah*, iv. 1.

Way of honour. The folio reading, altered by Malone to "ways."

Nor shall this peace. Those who believe that this play was written before the death of Elizabeth (see *Introduction*, p. 8) inclose in brackets the remainder of this speech and King Henry's "Thou speakest wonders," following it.

The maiden phœnix. See *Temp.* p. 132.

Wherever the bright sun, etc. See *Introduction*, p. 10. On a picture of King James, which formerly belonged to Bacon, and is now in the possession of Lord Grimston, he is styled *imperii Atlantici conditor* (Malone).

But she must die, etc. This paragraph reads thus in the folio:

> "But she must dye,
> She must, the Saints must haue her; yet a Virgin,
> A most vnspotted Lilly shall she passe
> To th' ground, and all the Worlde shall mourne her."

D. (followed by H.) thinks that Cranmer meant to express "regret at his foreknowledge that Elizabeth was to die *childless*, not that she was to *die*," and points the passage thus:

> "but she must die,—
> She must, the saints must have her,—yet a virgin;
> A most unspotted lily," etc.

But, as W. remarks, the archbishop simply means to say "that the Virgin Queen was too good to die."

Did I get anything. That is, anything worth reckoning in comparison with such a blessing.

And your good brethren. The folio has "And you good Brethren," which Theo. corrected, at the suggestion of Dr. Thirlby. The king would not call the aldermen his brethren.

Has business. That is, *he* has business. The folio reads "'Has businesse." See Gr. 400 and 461.

THE EPILOGUE.

On the authorship of the Epilogue, see notes on the Prologue.

Good women. The rhyme would seem to require that *women* be accented on the last syllable. Cf. Gr. 490.

If they smile, etc. Steevens remarks that we have the same thought in the Epilogues to *A. Y. L.* and 2 *Henry IV.*

ST. JAMES'S AND WESTMINSTER.

WESTMINSTER ABBEY.

INDEX OF WORDS EXPLAINED.

Aberga'ny, 161.
abhor (=*detestor*), 178.
abode (=bode), 159.
advertise (accent), 179.
afflictions (quadrisyllable), 182.
allay, 173.
Ampthill, 191.
Andren, 156.
angels (and *Angli*), 182.
an't, 170.
apostle spoons, 201.
Arde, 156.
Asher (=Esher), 186.
aspect (accent), 189.
attach (arrest), 161.
avaunt, 175.
avoid, 197.

banquet, 204.
been (omitted), 185.
beholding (=beholden), 169.
beshrew, 175.
Bevis, 157.
bevy, 169.
blistered (=puffed), 165.
Bohun, 172.
boldened, 162.
bombards, 205.
book (=learning), 159.
bore (=undermine), 160.
bowls, standing, 205.
brazier, 204.
break with, 197.

Campeius, 174.
can, 197.
Capucius, 196.
carry (=manage), 159, 163.
Cawood Castle, 193.
censure, 157.
certes, 158.
chambers (=guns), 9, 170.
Charter-house, 161.
Chartreux, 161.
chattels, 188.
cherubin, 157.
cheveril, 175.
chiding, 186.
chine, 203.

Cinque-ports, 193.
clerks (=clergy), 174.
clinquant, 157.
clubs, 204.
Clotharius, 165.
coast, 183.
Colbrand, 203.
collars of SS, 193.
colour (=pretext), 160.
compell'd (accent), 176.
complete (accent), 163, 183.
conceit, 176.
conceive, 163.
confederacy, 162.
confessor (accent), 164.
convent (=summon), 197.
cope (=encounter), 163.
corrupt (accent), 198.
covent (=convent), 195.

dare (larks), 187.
deliver (=relate), 163, 176.
demure, 164.
derive, 177.
device, 160.
discerner, 157.
Dunstable, 191.

Ego (*et rex meus*), 188.
element, 158.
emballing, 176.
envy (=malice), 172, 174, 182.
equal (=impartial), 174.
estate (=state), 174, 197.
even (=consistent), 182.
evils (=*foricæ*), 172.
exceeding (adverb), 196.
exclamation (=outcry), 162.

faint (=make faint), 176.
fierce (=extreme), 158.
file (=list), 158, 162.
file (verb), 185.
fire-drake, 204.
foot (=feet), 203.
for (=as), 177.
for (=as regards), 158, 173.
for (omitted), 172.
force (=hesitate), 195.

force (=urge), 183.
'fore, 178.
foresaid, 160.
forge, 164.
from (=of), 187.

gaping (=shouting), 203.
Garter, 193.
give way to, 183.
glistering, 175.
gossip, 205.
go to, 174.
guarded (=trimmed), 156.
Guy, Sir, 203.
Guynes, 156.

halidom, 198.
happily (=haply), 193.
happy (=favourable), 156.
hard (dissyllable), 184.
has (=he has), 166, 206.
have-at-him, 174.
having (=possession), 175, 185.
-head (=-hood), 175.
hedge, 183.
hire (dissyllable), 176.
hold (=hold good), 173.
hours (dissyllable), 197.
hull, 179.
husband (=manager), 185.

incense (=inform), 197.
indifferent (=impartial), 177.
indurance, 198.
innumerable (substance), 188.
instant (=present, passing), 161.
is (=are), 175.
issue (=son), 187.

jade, 187.
justify (=prove), 162.

keech, 158.
Kimbolton, 192.
knock (it), 170.

Leicester (Abbey), 193.
leisure, 185.
letters patents, 187.

level (=aim), 162.
lie (=reside), 192.
Limbo, 204.
Limbs of Limehouse, 204.
line (=equator), 204.
loose, 173.
long (=belong), 162, 176.
lop (noun), 163.

maidenhead, 175.
manage (noun), 200.
marry (=Mary), 159.
Marshalsea, 205.
may (=can), 179.
May-day, 203.
mean (=means), 201.
memorize, 183.
mere (=absolute), 188, 193.
mincing, 175.
mistaken, 160.
model (=image), 196.
motley, 156.
mount (=raise), 160, 164.
mumchance, 168.
music (=musicians), 193, 196.
mysteries, 165.

naughty (=wicked), 198.
needs, 173.
never so (=ever so), 165.
news, 173.
noise (=music), 203.
nothing (adverb), 198.

of (in adjurations), 182.
of (=from), 205.
of (omitted), 193.
of (=on, 184, 187.
omit (=neglect), 183.
once (=sometimes), 163.
one (the least), 178.
on't, 176.
open (=exposed), 173, 189.
opinion (=reputation), 156.
Orpheus, 181.
other (=anything else), 166.
out of, 190, 205.

pain (=pains), 184.
paned, 167.
panging, 175.
paper (verb), 158.
paragon (verb), 179.
Parish Garden, 202.
part (=depart), 182, 193.
part (=share), 199.
passages (=approaches), 178.
Paul's (pronunciation), 203.
peck, 205.
Pepin, 165.
period (=end), 164.
phisnomy, 167.
phœnix, 206.
pick, 205.
pillars (of a cardinal), 176, 190.
pinked, 204.
pitch (=height), 173.
place (=rank), 174, 178.
practice (=artifice), 160.
præmunire, 188.
prayers (dissyllable), 172.
prefer (=promote), 193.
presence (=presence-chamber), 181.
presence (=royal presence), 195.
present, at this, 200.
prime (=first), 185.
primer (=more urgent), 162.
primero, 197.
proper, 159.
putter-on, 162.

quarrel (=quarreler), 175.

rank, 164.
rate, 185.
refuse (=*recuso*), 178.
round (in the ear), 168.
royal (=loyal), 191.
rub, 173.

Saba, 206.
salute (my blood), 176.
sennet, 176.
set on, 180.
shall (=should), 163.
should, 186.
shrewd (=evil), 202.
sick (=ill-disposed), 163.
sign (=show), 178.
Sir Guy, 203.
so (=if), 159.
something (adverb), 160.
sometimes (=formerly), 179.
sooth, 175.
sound (=proclaim), 199.
spinster, 162.
spoons, apostle, 201.
SS, collars of, 193.
stand on, 198.
stand to, 178.
standing bowls, 205.
state (=estate), 174.
state (=throne), 162.
still (=ever), 175.
stir (against), 200.
stomach (=pride), 195.
strove (=striven), 177.
such which, 162.
suggest (=tempt), 160.
suggestion, 195.
superstitious, 182.

temperance (=patience), 160.
tendance, 185.
tender (=value), 178.
tennis, 165.
that (omitted), 181.
this (with plural noun), 189.
threepence (bowed), 175.
throughly, 197.
to (=against), 184.
to (=with), 204.
to (omitted and inserted), 177, 196.
tomb (of tears), 189.
trade, 197.
trembling, 163.
Tribulation of Tower Hill, 204.
trip, 196.

unhappily, 170.
unpartial, 174.
unwit, 185.
unwittingly, 185.
use (=interest), 190.

visitation (=visit), 160, 199.
visnomy, 167.
vizard, 196.

ween, 198.
weigh (=value), 198.
wench, 181.
which, the, 175, 178.
whiles, 198.
Whitehall, 166.
who (omitted), 178, 184.
whoever (=whomsoever), 172.
will (=would), 163.
wit (noun), 182.
wit (verb), 185.
with (=by), 193.
withal, 185.
witness, 198.
women (accent), 207.
worship, 157.
wot, 185.
wrought (=manœuvred), 188.

ye, 173, 182.
yet (transposed), 179.
York-place, 166.

THE END.

www.ingramcontent.com/pod-product-compliance
Lightning Source LLC
LaVergne TN
LVHW010741120826
845150LV00009B/1383